BIBLICAL MINISTRIES THROUGH WOMEN

God's Daughters
and
God's Work

Jack W. Hayford
with
M. Wendy Parrish

THOMAS NELSON PUBLISHERS
Nashville

CONTENTS

Biblical Ministries Through Women—God's Daughters and God's Work is one of a series of study guides that focus exciting, discovery-geared coverage of Bible book and power themes—all prompting toward dynamic, Holy Spirit-filled living.

About the Executive Editor

JACK W. HAYFORD, noted pastor, teacher, writer, and composer, is the Executive Editor of the complete series, working with the publisher in the conceiving and developing of each of the books.

Dr. Hayford is Senior Pastor of The Church On The Way, the First Foursquare Church of Van Nuys, California. He and his wife, Anna, have four married children, all of whom are active in either pastoral ministry or vital church life. As General Editor of the *Spirit-Filled Life Bible,* Pastor Hayford led a four-year project, which has resulted in the availability of one of today's most practical and popular study Bibles. He is author of more than twenty books, including *A Passion for Fullness, The Beauty of Spiritual Language, Rebuilding the Real You,* and *Prayer Is Invading the Impossible.* His musical compositions number over four hundred songs, including the widely sung "Majesty."

About the Writer

M. WENDY PARRISH is a wife and mother of three whose husband Frank is Senior Youth Pastor in one of California's largest churches. She studied at Pierce College in Los Angeles and at LIFE Bible College in San Dimas. Her background in church ministry is enriched, being the child of missionary parents, and her experience as a departmental director in graphic arts are only introductory features of those experiences that haved broadened her perspective on the challenges of today's Christian woman.

Wendy and Frank haved been married for twelve years and have three sons: Ben (11), Daniel (9), and Jonathan (8). The use of this study guide will be more thoroughly introduced to Wendy in the opening lesson, which refreshingly indicates the reason hosts of women will find an understanding friend in her.

Of this contributor, the Executive Editor has remarked, "Wendy Parrish is one of the most quietly dynamic young women I have ever met. The test of years of acquaintance has proven the validity of my observation: here is a gifted, godly, unusually graced lady—with a servant spirit to all."

THE KEYS
THAT KEEP ON FREEING

Is there anything that holds more mystery or more genuine practicality than a key? The mystery: "What does it fit? What can it turn on? What might it open? What new discovery could be made? The practicality: Something *will* most certainly open to the possessor! Something *will* absolutely be found to unlock and allow a possibility otherwise obstructed!

- Keys describe the instruments we use to access or ignite.
- Keys describe the concepts that unleash mind-boggling possibilities.
- Keys describe the different structures of musical notes which allow variation and range.

Jesus spoke of keys: "And I will give you the keys of the kingdom of heaven, and whatever you bind on earth will be bound in heaven, and whatever you loose on earth will be loosed in heaven" (Matt. 16:19).

While there is no conclusive list of exactly what keys Jesus was referring to, it is clear that He did confer upon His church—upon *all* who believe—the access to a realm of spiritual partnership with Him in the dominion of His kingdom. Faithful students of the Word of God, moving in the practical grace and biblical wisdom of Holy Spirit-filled living and ministry, have noted some of the primary themes which undergird this order of "spiritual partnership" Christ offers. The "keys" are *concepts*—biblical themes that are traceable through the Scriptures and verifiably dynamic when applied with soundly based faith under the lordship of Jesus Christ. The "partnership" is the *essential* feature of this release of divine grace;

(1) believers reaching to *receive* Christ's promise of "kingdom keys," (2) while choosing to *believe* in the Holy Spirit's readiness to actuate their unleashing, unlimited power today.

Companioned with the Bible book studies in the *Spirit-Filled Life Study Guide* series, the Kingdom Dynamic studies present a dozen different themes. This study series is an outgrowth of the Kingdom Dynamics themes included throughout the *Spirit-Filled Life Bible,* which provide a treasury of insight developed by some of today's most respected Christian leaders. From that beginning, studious writers have evolved the elaborated studies you'll pursue here.

The central goal of the subjects focused on in this present series of study guides is to relate "power points" of the Holy Spirit-filled life. Assisting you in your discoveries are a number of helpful features. Each study guide has twelve to fourteen lessons, each arranged so you can plumb the depths or skim the surface, depending upon your needs and interests. The study guides contain major lesson features, each marked by a symbol and heading for easy identification.

 WORD WEALTH

The WORD WEALTH feature provides important definitions of key terms.

 BEHIND THE SCENES

BEHIND THE SCENES supplies information about cultural beliefs and practices, doctrinal disputes, business trades, and the like, that illuminate Bible passages and teachings.

AT A GLANCE

The AT A GLANCE feature uses maps and charts to identify places and simplify themes or positions.

 KINGDOM EXTRA

Because this study guide focuses on a theme of the Bible, you will find a KINGDOM EXTRA feature that guides you into Bible dictionaries, Bible encyclopedias, and other resources that will enable you to glean more from the Bible's wealth on the topic if you want something extra.

 PROBING THE DEPTHS

Another feature, PROBING THE DEPTHS, will explain controversial issues raised by particular lessons and cite Bible passages and other sources to which you can turn to help you come to your own conclusions.

 FAITH ALIVE

Finally, each lesson contains a FAITH ALIVE feature. Here the focus is, So what? Given what the Bible says, what does it mean for my life? How can it impact my day-to-day needs, hurts, relationships, concerns, and whatever else is important to me? FAITH ALIVE will help you see and apply the practical relevance of God's literary gift.

As you'll see, these guides supply space for you to answer the study and life-application questions and exercises. You may, however, want to record all your answers, or just the overflow from your study or application, in a separate notebook or journal. This would be especially helpful if you think you'll dig into the KINGDOM EXTRA features. Because the exercises in this feature are optional and can be expanded as far as you want to take them, we have not allowed writing space for them in this study guide. So you may want to have a notebook or journal handy for recording your discoveries while working through to this feature's riches.

The Bible study method used in this series revolves around four basic steps: observation, interpretation, correlation, and application. Observation answers the question, What does the text say? Interpretation deals with, What does the text mean? —not with what it means to you or me, but what it meant to its original readers. Correlation asks, What light do other Scripture passages shed on this text? And application, the goal of Bible study, poses the question, How should my life change in response to the Holy Spirit's teaching of this text?

If you have used a Bible much before, you know that it comes in a variety of translations and paraphrases. Although you can use any of them with profit as you work through the *Spirit-Filled Life Kingdom Dynamics Study Guide* series, when Bible passages or words are cited, you will find they are from the New King James Version of the Bible. Using this translation with this series will make your study easier, but it's certainly not necessary.

The only resources you need to complete and apply these study guides are a heart and mind open to the Holy Spirit, a prayerful attitude, and a pencil and a Bible. Of course, you may draw upon other sources, such as commentaries, dictionaries, encyclopedias, atlases, and concordances, and you'll even find some optional exercises that will guide you into these sources. But these are extras, not necessities. These study guides are comprehensive enough to give you all you need to gain a good, basic understanding of the Bible book being covered and how you can apply its themes and counsel to your life.

A word of warning, though. By itself, Bible study will not transform your life. It will not give you power, peace, joy, comfort, hope, and a number of other gifts God longs for you to unwrap and enjoy. Through Bible study, you will grow in your understanding of the Lord, His kingdom and your place in it, and those things are essential. But you need more. You need to rely on the Holy Spirit to guide your study and your application of the Bible's truths. He, Jesus promised, was sent to teach us "all things" (John 14:26; cf. 1 Cor. 2:13). So as you use this series to guide you through Scripture, bathe your study time in prayer, asking the Spirit of God to illuminate the text, enlighten your mind, humble your will, and comfort your heart. He will never let you down.

My prayer and goal for you is that as you unlock and begin to explore God's Book for living His way, the Holy Spirit will fill every fiber of your being with the joy and power God longs to give all His children. So read on. Be diligent. Stay open and submissive to Him. You will not be disappointed. He promises you!

Lesson 1/God's Daughter and God's Daughters

I have been invited, by reason of the unique nature of this book, to take a few moments to tell you about myself, and then introduce you to the lessons this guide contains.

First of all, I am a daughter, a sister, a stepdaughter, a wife, a granddaughter, a mother, a stepsister, an aunt and a daughter-in-law. And not necessarily in that order! How many of those do we share in common? Perhaps you're even fortunate enough to add one I can't (yet)—a grandmother. In other words, I'm a woman, just like you.

I have lived alone and wondered if life was passing me by; now I am married and wonder if life is passing me by. I enjoy the privilege of raising three sons, and the agony of hoping I do it right. I grew up in a "functional family" that sometimes wasn't. I attended both secular and Christian colleges but didn't graduate from either. I had to adjust to life in a foreign nation, where my husband and I pioneered a church. And right when I'd finally settled in, we came back. I managed an office while trying to manage a household. Now, I manage a household while not managing much else! I had a wonderful mom, whom I loved and lost, far too soon, to cancer. I dreaded a step-family, but was pleasantly surprised. I've learned to "be not angry without a cause," while hoping my husband had one for working so late. I've prayed for unsaved family members and prayed with other family members. I've wondered how God could ever use my life and been terrified that He might actually want to. I've loved, lost, hoped, feared, laughed, cried, sung, worried, cared, envied, dreamed, and despaired. In other words, I really am a woman just like you.

God, through His Word, has given us the opportunity to meet for ourselves many other women just like you and me, who experienced many of the same challenges, joys, and anxieties that we do today. This lesson will allow a glimpse at the women you'll meet as you journey through *Biblical Ministries Through Women*. Though you may not have enough information to answer each question completely, write at least as much as you can. This will help prepare you for your encounters with each of the characters later on in the study. And remember, be as honest with your answers as possible. This is not a test, and the point is not "right answers"; the point is the discovery of truth.

Turn in your Bible to Genesis 12 and read verses 1–9. How would you feel if your husband told you that tomorrow you would pack everything you owned and move, but he didn't know the destination yet? (Remember, be honest!)

According to just those nine verses, at how many different places did Abraham and Sarah stop? (vv. 1–9)

What do you think Sarah was thinking by the time they were heading south toward Egypt? (v. 9)

Now read Genesis 12:10–20. Why do you think Sarah went along with Abraham's suggestion?

Do you think she was also guilty of the deception for agreeing to Abraham's plan? Why or why not?

Is there a point where submission is wrong? Or is the topic of submission even a relevant issue anymore?

Now read Genesis 16:1–6. Why did Sarah give her maid Hagar to Abraham?

This created tension between Hagar and Sarah (v. 4). What did Sarah do to Hagar? (v. 6)

Given the situation Hagar had been put in, how do you think she was feeling?

Continue in your Bible to Genesis 18:9–12. Sarah, at this point, was 89 years old. What was the Lord's promise to her? (v. 10)

What was her response? (v. 12)

Is doubt in God's promises wrong?

What would your reaction be if God said the same thing to you today?

When does our faith require action, and when do we "let go and let God"?

Are there situations too hard even for God?

While on the topic of things being hard for God, turn in your Bible to Genesis 3:1–7. What was Eve's gravest error?

How do you think Eve's story relates to having faith in God's promises?

Look at Genesis 25:21–23. What did the Lord tell Rebekah regarding her twins?

Now read Genesis 27:1–40. In light of what God had said to Rebekah, did the end justify the means? Was she right in what she did, or did it actually show a lack of faith?

In regard to faith, would you have the faith to say "yes" to God if He were to direct you to lead tens of thousands of women in worship?

Turn to Exodus 15:20, 21. Who was afforded that privilege?

What additional office of ministry did she hold? (v. 20)

Look now at 2 Kings 22:13–20. From whom did Hilkiah and Shaphan seek counsel and God's wisdom?

From what source did she speak? (vv. 15, 16)

Now turn to 1 Corinthians 14:34. Did ministry possibilities like those of Huldah and Miriam end for women in the New Testament?

Read Acts 18:25, 26 and Romans 16:3–5. Is ministry only proper for women outside the church or when partnered with a husband?

Miriam was an influential woman in ministry. But, unfortunately, she gave in to her flesh and displeased the Lord. According to Numbers 12:1, 2, what did she do?

Why did her actions anger the Lord? (12:6–9)

Is it ever appropriate to criticize those God places in authority?

How important are the things a woman says?

In Judges 4 we read of a woman who spoke and led with wisdom. Who was she? (v. 4)

Under what condition would Barak heed her counsel? (v. 8)

Would you be willing to act as courageously as Deborah on a matter of personal conviction?

For more reading on another woman of conviction, turn to Ruth 2 and read verses 1–3. What was Ruth doing? (v. 3)

Why were she and Naomi in that position in the first place? (1:3–5)

What importance does the Lord attach to the mundane tasks of daily survival?

Can you think of a scripture to support your answer?

From where did Ruth draw the strength and courage to face her difficult trial?

Now read Ruth 3:1–4. What do you think of Naomi's advice to Ruth?

What was Ruth's response? (v. 5)

What did Ruth mean when she asked Boaz to "take your maidservant under your wing"? (v. 9)

What is a kinsman-redeemer, and how does that relate to you today?

Things ended up working together for good in Ruth's case. Turn now to Romans 8:28. What does the Bible mean by "*His* purpose"?

For more on a woman's purpose, turn to the Book of Esther. Read 1:10–19. Why was the queen's position vacated?

Does that seem harsh or unfair to you?

Who filled the vacancy, and how was she chosen? (2:12–17)

Esther risked her life and future for the sake of her people. What did Mordecai ask that provided the catalyst for her courageous deeds? (4:14)

How did fasting help prepare Esther for what she was about to attempt? (4:16)

What role did faith play in Esther's life? (4:16, 17)

Esther was an orphan who eventually became a revered queen. How do you think she managed to keep her priorities clear in the midst of such opulence and notoriety?

What can you learn from Esther's life about the purpose of God for you?

The Bible makes no mention of Esther desiring or having children. But for many women in Scripture it was of vital concern. And for one woman, her role as mother changed the course of eternity. Turn to Luke 1 and read verses 26–38. What sacrifices did Mary have to make before Jesus was even born?

What was Mary's response to what was being required of her? (v. 38)

Now turn to 2 Timothy 1:5, 6. What do you perceive about the influence of a mother's faith on her children?

Does God make provision for single moms or those with unbelieving husbands?

What is shown about the nature of God through the mothers of Scripture?

Turn to Matthew 14:6–11. How can a mother's impure motives influence her children?

Are there important principles that apply to any woman, whether or not they've given birth, that can be learned from the mothers of the Bible?

Would that also apply to the ministry of wives? Can any woman glean from the lessons of Proverbs 31? Give at least two examples of truths from that passage that would apply to any believing woman.

How are women asked to respond to their husbands in Ephesians 5:33?

What if he makes that really hard to do? Turn to 1 Samuel 25 and read verses 1–38. Why do you think Abigail didn't just let Nabal reap the judgment of David?

What is God's intended purpose for wives?

What about for women in general? How can we serve Him from our "Jerusalem" (Acts 1:8), from the place of our most immediate influence?

Turn to Acts 16 and read verses 13–15. How did Lydia express her gratitude to Paul and his fellow travelers?

Why do you think true hospitality is such a rare and unusual thing today?

How did Jesus feel about hospitality? Read Matthew 10:40–42.

How extravagant does the extension of hospitality need to be? (v. 42)

Turn to Genesis 24 and read verses 10–60. Was this a one-time incident, or are there blessings that can result from being hospitable?

Is the level of intimacy and openness experienced through the sharing of a meal different from that experienced through conversation? Explain.

This lesson has provided a peek into the lives of just a few of God's daughters. Would you like to know more about them? to glean from their experiences? to see how God used their lives? to grow from their faith? I trust you would, and I hope this guide assists you in doing so.

One important thing to keep in mind is that these lessons barely scratch the surface of some very deep and difficult issues. They are not intended to be exhaustive or to lead you to all the "correct" conclusions; but they should stir you, inspire you, convict you, and perhaps even provoke you into further examination and discovery of God's Word. And, hopefully, they will bring a discerning of the mind and intentions of the heart (Heb. 4:12).

It's been my privilege to meet you. Allow me, if you will, the honor of leading you to the feasting table of God's Word. And once you've tasted of the King's bounty, I trust you'll receive His invitation to return as often as you can.

Yours in His service,
M. Wendy Parrish

Lesson 2/Sarah—Daughter of Faith: The Triumph

Hebrews 11:1 states, "Now faith is the substance of things hoped for, the evidence of things not seen." It is in this same chapter of Hebrews, so aptly describing how faith works, that we find Sarah listed as an example of one who, along with her husband Abraham, excelled in faith. In so doing, she saw God miraculously intervene on her behalf and use her life to further His will. We will examine how her faith endured through many transitions, failures, difficult points of submission, and heartbreaking trials. Though beautiful, Sarah did not rely on the outward appearance (1 Pet. 3:3, 4), but displayed great character, grace, dignity, and courage. We can discover much from the life of Sarah that will help us walk in the triumph of faith.

First, read Genesis 11:27—23:2 for an overview of the life of Sarah, at least as much as is recorded in Scripture. Write down any questions or observations that you have as you read.

 PROBING THE DEPTHS

Setting the historical stage gives us a better understanding of why people responded as they did, prevents misinterpretation or misapplication of Scripture, and can also show us a pattern of God's dealings. If you have further background and cultural questions after this study, they can be answered through study Bibles, reference books, and Bible concordances or encyclopedias. Check with your pastor or a nearby Christian college library for titles and authors. For more about Sarah, you could begin with Ur, the longtime home Abraham and Sarah were asked to leave behind.

It will enhance our study to learn more about Abraham and Sarah as a couple. First, you'll notice their names early on were Abram, meaning "Exalted Father," and Sarai, "Princess." Turn to Genesis 17:1–22 and read of God's covenant with Abram. It was at this time that God, as a sign of His established covenant, changed Abram to Abraham, "Father of a Multitude," and Sarai became Sarah, "the princess," or "Queen." [NOTE: For ease of reference, we will refer to them throughout this study by their God-given names, Abraham and Sarah.]

KINGDOM EXTRA

Genesis 11:29 contains the Bible's first mention of Sarah as Abraham's wife. This was approximately 2100 B.C. For more on how this date was arrived at, check reference materials containing surveys of Israel's history.

Though there is not much information about her early years, we do know something of Sarah's heritage. Read Genesis 20:12, then Genesis 11:26. Who was Sarah's father?

Besides marriage, how then were Abraham and Sarah related?

We make note of their relationship because it will be important later in our study. Also note that this type of marriage was common "in tightly knit societies, such as those of the patriarchal age,"[1] and occurred sometimes for religious reasons (Gen. 24:3, 4; 28:1, 2).

According to Genesis 17:17, what was their difference in age?

Though we are not privy to many intimate conversations between Abraham and Sarah, the Bible does narrate several scenes that help us form a picture of what their relationship may have been like. Look at Genesis 12:5, as Abraham and Sarah are departing Haran. First, list all that they took.

Does it appear from this that Abraham was sensitive to a wife's desires? Why or why not?

Now read Genesis 16:1, 2. Do you think Abraham respected Sarah's opinions? Give reasons for your answer.

Look further at Genesis 16:6. What phrase tells you that Abraham trusted Sarah's judgment?

Turn now to 1 Peter 3:3–6. What does the Bible record as Sarah's attitude toward her husband?

Page back to Genesis 23:2, and record what Abraham's reaction to his loss of Sarah tells you about their relationship.

FAITH IN TRANSITION

As the story of Sarah begins, she is in the process of transition, or moving—an event that becomes a common one throughout her life. Although, hopefully, few of us will ever move so often, there is something of the application of faith in the midst of transition that can apply to all of us; for we will all, in some form or another, face the challenge of leaving a place of familiarity in our lives for some unknown "destination," wherein we have only the leading of God through the Holy Spirit, or the leading of someone in authority over us, to trust.

Read Genesis 11:31 and record the circumstances and destination of Sarah's first uprooting from Ur.

BEHIND THE SCENES

Historians have discovered Ur was a place of culture and commerce, enjoying considerable affluence. It maintained harbors where goods from the east were exchanged for local crops. The middle-class homes were two-story; a system of formal education was in place; perhaps only Egypt had more skilled craftsmen.

By its description, Ur appears to have been a nice place to live, given the standards of the day. Think for a moment about all that Sarah was being asked to forgo in leaving her home, relatives, and familiar associations. Write out what you think her feelings might have been, and why.

Now read Genesis 12:1 and Hebrews 11:8. At this point, Sarah has lost her father-in-law, is still childless, and is 65 years old (comparing her life span with today's, she was right at the midpoint of her life); and she and Abraham are moving again. According to the above verses, where and when was their final destination?

How do you think Sarah felt about this "destination"?

Though it's likely that Abraham shared with her of God's leading, do you think this move was a challenge to Sarah's faith? Why?

What would be your response if you were given a similar set of circumstances? (Joy, anger, fear, anticipation, dread, hope, anxiety, excitement—choose from these, or add your own.)

   AT A GLANCE

Now review Abraham and Sarah's 1,500-mile journey by following the route indicated on the map below.

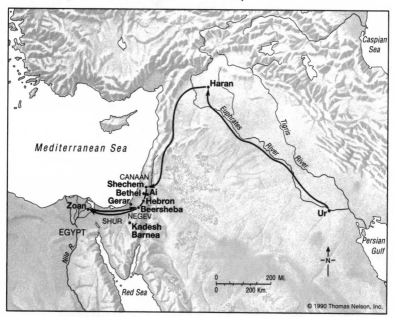

Abraham's Journey of Faith. Abraham's 1,500-mile journey was fueled by faith. "And he went out, not knowing where he was going. By faith he dwelt in the land of promise as *in* a foreign country, . . . for he waited for the city which has foundations, whose builder and maker is God" (Heb. 11:8–10).[2]

BEHIND THE SCENES

Keep in mind that Abraham and Sarah went from being city-dwellers to being seminomads. They either walked or rode donkeys or camels through the dry, semidesert, along the Euphrates River, and around the Mediterranean Sea. Their food was likely dried figs and dates, parched grains, dried olives, and breads they would make along the way. It was certainly no pleasure trip!

KINGDOM EXTRA

For more details, refer to books on biblical culture, or reference materials that contain information on the manners and customs of Bible times.

It appears, given no record of contention or disunity, that Sarah *trusted* Abraham's leading through all these difficult transitions. But it also appears her trust went beyond Abraham. Look again at 1 Peter 3:5. What does the Bible say was the basis of her submission to Abraham?

First Peter 3:6 tells us Sarah was unafraid of obedience to Abraham. Why do you think this was so?

To what, then, would you attribute Sarah's amazing level of faith through difficult transitions? (Be as thorough and specific as you can.)

Notice that Abraham and Sarah did not know *why* they had to leave, *where* they were going, *when* they would get there, or *how* God intended to fulfill His promise. They could only trust in "*what* they knew about *Whom* they knew!"

FAITH ALIVE

Read 2 Samuel 22:1–4; Psalm 37:3–5; Proverbs 3:5, 6; 16:20; Jeremiah 17:7, 8; and Nahum 1:7. What can you take from Sarah's experience and the scriptures you've studied and apply to your own life when it comes to times of difficult change or transition?

FAITH THROUGH SUBMISSION

Read Genesis 12:10–20 and Genesis 20:1–18. Write down your observations or questions regarding these two passages (remember: be honest!).

These events can seem absolutely amazing, totally bewildering, and unbelievably astounding! How could Sarah, our model of faith, do what Abraham asked of her in these instances? And what compelled Abraham, father of nations (Gen. 17:5) and friend of God (2 Chr. 20:7), to ask her to do such a thing? And what was God's response to all this?

Let's begin with Sarah. Although she was imperfect, and, as we'll soon discover, acted rashly on occasion, the Bible never records a single instance of her disobeying her husband. For that, she is praised in 1 Peter 3:6. To aid our understanding, let us examine the words "submissive" and "obeyed," as they relate to this verse in 1 Peter.

WORD WEALTH

Submissive, *hupotasso.* From *hupo,* under; and *tasso,* an orderly manner, appoint. Literally, "to stand under."
We see a place of protection and freedom for wives, as they "come under the appointment" (or charge) given to a husband by God. *As a husband aligns himself with God's*

order and receives God's *appointment* to be a covering for his wife (Gen. 3:16; Eph. 5:23–33), he also comes under God's covering. So in standing under the protective covering of her husband, a wife is also under the larger umbrella of the covering of God. By stepping out from either, she steps out from both.

WORD WEALTH

Obeyed, *hupakouo.* To hear as a subordinate, listen attentively, obey as a subject, answer and respond, submit without reservation. *Hupakouo* was used particularly of servants who were attentive to the requests made of them and who complied. This word thus contains the ideas of hearing, responding, and obeying.[3]

So, even without the benefit of the written Word of God, Sarah understood the wisdom of complying with God's order. (Given their knowledge of God, one wouldn't be surprised if Abraham and Sarah had been recipients of the stories of history, including Adam and Eve and God's command of Genesis 3:16). She also was clearly not a victim of an insensitive, suppressive "master," but was under the canopy of a loving husband who, as we have seen, respected and cared for her.

But would Sarah have been justified in these two incidents if she had refused to go along with Abraham's plan? Wasn't she also guilty of the deception by participating? Yes, she probably was. And she may have been wiser to refuse to participate. Record what you think she should have done.

One could argue that Sarah believed Abraham was being led by God in what he asked her to do. "[Sarah] was indeed his half sister, as we learn from 20:12. But she was his 'sister' in another manner also: [Abraham] had just come from Haran, with its custom of 'adopting' one's wife as sister in order to confer special privileges, including inheritance, upon her. Nonetheless, it was deceptive, unnecessary, and faithless."[4]

Perhaps Sarah, afraid for her loving husband, agreed in order to save his life. Or maybe she was simply acting out of obedience to her husband. In any case, an amazing thing takes place. Read Genesis 12:17–20. In this account, Sarah is added to the concubines of the Pharaoh. How do you think she was feeling right about then?

Abraham's decision obviously put Sarah in a difficult situation and God did not prevent that. But what did He do for Sarah? (12:18–20)

Now read Genesis 20:2–18. Why do you think Sarah agreed to Abraham's plan again? (v. 13)

Does verse 5 show any sign of resistance on Sarah's part?

What did God do specifically for Sarah on this occasion? (vv. 3, 6, 7, 18)

Whom does Abimelech rebuke? (vv. 9, 10)

"Abimelech was both terrified and angry. He gave large gifts in order to gain favor with God and with Abraham. Verse 16 is difficult, but the meaning is nevertheless clear: 'Here is compensation for any injury to your personal honor.'"[5]

According to 20:17, what did Abraham do?

Do you think there might have been any repentance involved on Abraham's part?

Is there evidence in scripture of this kind of situation ever happening again to Sarah?

In these accounts we see exemplified the wonderful truth about God and His divine order of submission. It does not depend upon the qualifications or infallibility of man; only upon the faithfulness and sovereignty of God! Because Sarah was, as an act of faith, in submission to her husband, and was in alignment with God's order, and so under His canopy (see "Probing the Depths" below), she was then a candidate for the full measure of God's protection and blessing. By choosing to remain under her husband's leadership, even when in weakness he stumbled and opened his wife to harm, it was God who intervened on Sarah's behalf, because of the position of her heart. And they actually ended up better off than when they began (see Gen. 20:14–16).

What do you think about Sarah's choice? In the light of the fruit of her faith, is there a lesson for today's woman?

PROBING THE DEPTHS

To better understand the Word of God and its directives regarding God's order for a wife, see Ephesians 5:22–24, Colossians 3:18, and 1 Peter 3:1–6 (it is also addressed further in later lessons).

Even in the case of the unbelieving husband, God's principles still apply if the husband will continue to live with her (1 Cor. 7:13–15). A woman "is told that her 'words' are not her key to success in winning her husband to Christ; but her Christlike, loving spirit is"[6] (1 Pet. 3:1–6).

Now let's turn to Genesis 16 to another woman's situation. Read the entire chapter and for now, let us look at Hagar. (We will study Sarah's actions in the next lesson.)

Here was an innocent maid simply fulfilling her role as the law allowed at that time and obeying the directives as given to her. But suddenly she was being treated unrighteously and unfairly because of it.

Read Genesis 16:6 and record Hagar's response to Sarah's treatment of her.

The Angel of the Lord found her and, in verse 8, addressed her. Write down what He said to her.

It is interesting to note that this divine address established the right priority from the start. Although Hagar was treated imperfectly, it was apparently not an excuse to step out from God's order.

 FAITH ALIVE

It is a tremendous thing to realize the importance God places on adherence to His divine order. In Genesis 16:13, Hagar calls the Lord, "The-God-Who-Sees." He saw her in a place of despair and hopelessness, and she was not forgotten (we will look at this further in the next lesson). But He also saw her through His eyes, and addressed her as such.

We may think of ourselves as many things (for example, wife of . . . , mother of . . . , employee of . . .), but have we put them in the order of priority as God sees them? If God were to speak to you TODAY, how would *He* address you? What would be your #1 position or priority through His eyes?

It is important to note that this study in no way suggests that a woman should subject herself to harm or abuse in the name of submission; and a husband is charged to not exploit a wife's trust (Eph. 5:25–29; 1 Pet. 3:7). But it is also important to note that a loving wife, with the incorruptible beauty of a gentle and quiet spirit, is precious not only to her husband (Prov. 31:10, 11), but also in the sight of God (1 Pet. 3:4).

Summarize this section on "Faith Through Submission" by answering the thought questions we asked in the beginning of this lesson.

How could Sarah do what Abraham asked?

What compelled Abraham to ask her to do such a thing?

What was God's response to all this?

The principle of submission is a challenge to anyone's flesh and grates against the very nature of our human tendencies. It is particularly difficult for women because of the confusion and misapplication of the truth that has existed regarding the subject. But remember that "submission" is a clear principle established by God out of His all-wise, all-loving omniscience for our protection and blessing. And real freedom, the genuine liberation to be all God intends us to be, can only come through the knowledge of genuine truth (John 8:31, 32), and the application, or living out, of that truth in one's personal life (James 1:22–25). It is in that place of trust in God and His order for our lives that we can walk in the triumph of faith.

As you conclude this section on "Faith Through Submission," take a few moments and review the study on Sarah and submission. *In your own words*, while applying the truth of God's Word, write a definition of submission. Be as thorough as you can.

 FAITH ALIVE

Think about all those in your life who are in some place of authority over you (a pastor, an employer, the Lord). List as many as come to mind in a column below. In light of what

God is teaching you about submission, write next to each one the ways you can adjust your relationship with them in order to better align yourself under their covering. Use a Bible concordance to find a scripture reference to support your "adjustments."

Example:

person	needed adjustments	reference
my husband	-treat him with more respect	-Eph. 5:33
	-trust his leading	-1 Pet. 3:6

REMEMBER: Christ can enable us to fulfill these desires and walk in a manner pleasing to God but we *must* ask of Him what we need. Take time to prayerfully lift this list to God that He might grant you everything necessary to live a released life of "Faith Through Submission."

FAITH REQUIRES ACTION

Though Sarah was not always consistent in her walk of faith (which we will look at more closely in the next lesson), in Hebrews 11:11 she is heralded for her faith. Read that passage. It is apparent that just believing something can happen is not always enough. Faith often demands an action on our part. Though Abraham and Sarah may have passed the age where they had relations, what action was required of Sarah to fulfill God's promise?

According to James 2:14–24, summarize the importance of a faith that takes action.

There is a very fine line between partnership with God for the release of His promise and deciding to help God by taking matters into our own hands. Though faith requires action, it should always be strictly in line with God's promises through His Word. An extreme example might be found in a woman believing God has a marriage partner for her. In her impatience, she finds a nice man, but he's not a believer. She justifies the union, while ignoring the full counsel of God (2 Cor. 6:14, 15), and much pain and heartache result. (Read Genesis 21:21, which records Hagar's securing a wife for Ishmael from the idolatrous Egyptians, contrary to God's promise and directives.)

 ### FAITH ALIVE

Perhaps you've recognized an area in your own life where your passive faith needs to take on a more aggressive action. Wishing for something will not make it happen, but consistent prayer can release it. Just wanting to forgive may not bring release; but choosing, by an act of your will, to forgive and deciding to let go of a wrong committed against you will bring freedom. Record below a promise of God for which you are believing. Now prayerfully ask the Lord what action of partnership He would have you take for the release of His promise (record that also).

Write down any other questions this study has brought to mind or additional conclusions you'd like to make.

1. *Spirit-Filled Life Bible* (Nashville, TN: Thomas Nelson Publishers, 1991), 34, note on 20:12.

2. Ibid., map on 23.

3. Ibid, 1696, "Word Wealth: 6:17 obeyed."

4. Ibid., 23, note on 12:11–13.

5. Ibid., 34, note on 20:14–18.

6. Ibid., 1912, "Kingdom Dynamics: A Word of Wisdom to Wives."

Lesson 3/Sarah—Daughter of Faith: The Trial

In the first lesson, we examined the virtues of Sarah's faith, and her steadfast trust in God. But Sarah, like us, was only flesh, and faltered at times in her walk of faith.

There are vital lessons throughout Scripture that teach us the godly response to various trials or circumstances. But also included in God's Word are examples of failure, accompanied by the redemption of God, His judgment, or the natural result of sin. Since *all* of Scripture is inspired by God, and is "profitable for doctrine, for reproof, for correction, for instruction in righteousness" (2 Tim. 3:16), there is evidently as much to learn from the failures of people as from the successes.

Thus, let us examine several occasions when Sarah and others went beyond godly action through faith and took matters into their own hands. Let us also consider the consequences of their failure to trust the full promise of God.

Read Genesis 11:30 for an introduction to what was probably the greatest challenge to Sarah and her faith in God.

 BEHIND THE SCENES

Bearing a child was central to the identity of a Hebrew woman. Producing an heir was part of the marriage vows. God Himself had commanded His people to be fruitful and multiply (Gen. 1:28). In ancient Israel, a child was considered part of God's blessing, and the lack of a child was thought to be His curse (Deut. 28:1–4, 15–18).

We have already examined in Genesis 12—14 Sarah's faithful response to God's dealings with Abraham and her willingness to follow his leading. As the years passed, they experienced blessing and provision, but, to Sarah's sorrow, were still childless. This was confusing even to Abraham (15:2). *"How does this reckon with [God's] promise?* is Abram's complaint."[1]

Read Genesis 15. Summarize the covenant God makes with Abraham.

🚪 BEHIND THE SCENES

In verse 2, Abraham is referring to the fact that "culture permitted a senior slave to become heir to a childless man."[2]

In light of Sarah's response to God's dealings with Abraham thus far, what do you think her initial reaction to this covenant may have been?

As many as ten years pass, and Sarah allows a seed of doubt to land in the soil of her heart. Granted, all the natural circumstances gave her reason to wonder about God's promises. But had she already forgotten God's supernatural intervention on her behalf? Read Genesis 12:14–20 to review God's faithfulness to Sarah. Write out verse 17 below.

Sarah allowed the seed of doubt to remain, and it grew to unbelief. She decided God needed her help and took matters into her own hands. According to Genesis 16:1–3, what did Sarah decide to do?

This act, not the doubt, was her first failure. Read Mark 9:14–27, and summarize the account.

What were Jesus' words to the man in verse 23?

What was the man's response to what Jesus said to him? (v. 24)

Doubt, then, is understandable. But rather than cry out to God for help at her point of doubt, the failure of Sarah was in allowing the doubt to remain and grow to unbelief, which led her to act according to the flesh, apart from God (Gal. 4:23).

Abraham had his own times of doubting the power of God to sustain Sarah and him and to fulfill His word to them (Gen. 12; 20), and he also took matters into his own hands. Perhaps that is what opened the door to Sarah's faithless plan.

Was this a time when Sarah could have thought and done differently from her husband? Explain.

Who was now pulled into Sarah's plan? (Gen. 16:1–4)

BEHIND THE SCENES

This new character in the story, as Sarah's personal maid, was likely a favorite servant in the large household. Ironically, she was a symbol of God's provision and protection for Sarah, as she was probably a gift from Pharaoh (Gen. 12:16, 20).

PROBING THE DEPTHS

The presence of a concubine was common in those times, particularly when someone was needed to produce an heir. For more on the laws concerning concubines, read Exodus 21:7–11, Leviticus 19:20–22, and Deuteronomy 21:10–14. Many Old Testament figures had concubines, including Jacob (Gen. 30:4), Gideon (Judg. 8:31), Saul (2 Sam. 3:7), David (2 Sam. 5:13; 15:16), and Solomon (1 Kin. 11:3).

So though it was within Sarah's legal right to give Hagar to Abraham, what do you think it expressed regarding her understanding of and faith in God's promise to Abraham?

Sarah then gave Hagar to Abraham. Given what we know of their relationship, this must have been a difficult and painful decision. The sacrifice was great, but it was *not* one God was asking her to make. Turn to Proverbs 21:3 and write what the Lord values even more than our sacrifice.

As it happens with unbelief, Sarah's doubt also began to affect those around her. What was Abraham's response to Sarah's faithless plan? (Gen. 16:2)

FAITH ALIVE

Think of a time when you were going through a trial of faith, and someone expressed doubt or unbelief to you. How did it make you feel?

Did it change the outcome of your decisions in the midst of the trial? Or did it affect your faith?

What can you learn about offering suggestions or advice when someone is going through a difficult test of faith?

Hagar conceives, but her now-haughty attitude (16:5) stabs again at a difficult issue for Sarah—her pride. It is pride that causes one to challenge the validity of God's Word (Gen. 3:1–5). It was pride that led Sarah to cover her embarrassment and provide herself with an heir; and it was likely the same pride, coupled with her own feelings of inadequacy, that caused her now to despise Hagar.

How is pride contrary to faith?

There is no doubt Sarah was already regretting her decision to take matters into her own hands. As with all things done in the flesh, they seem so enticing and clever at the time; but the negative results can snowball quickly.

How do you think Sarah's plan changed the atmosphere in her home?

Sarah even began to point fingers. Whom did she blame in Genesis 16:5?

Why do you think she did that?

In verse 6, Sarah's frustration made matters even worse. What happened?

Though the action was forbidden for a bondwoman, what did Hagar apparently think was the easiest solution? (v. 6)

What did the Angel of the Lord require Hagar to do? (v. 9)

God gave an accompanying promise in verse 10. What was it?

Record Hagar's response (v. 13).

BEHIND THE SCENES

Hagar bore Abraham a son, Ishmael (16:16). The results of Sarah's pride and impatience carried consequences far greater than even she could have imagined, for the descendants of Ishmael (the Arabs) and the descendants of Isaac (the Jews) have to this day remained bitter enemies. An important lesson for us is the far-reaching effects of taking a seat in God's throne and attempting to direct our own destinies contrary to His Word.

Genesis 17 records the appearance of the Lord to Abraham when he was 99 years old, and His affirmation of the covenant, which this time specifically addressed Sarah. What were God's directives concerning her in verses 15 and 16?

How did Abraham react? (v. 17)

Besides the fact that God did not rebuke him, how do verses 23–27 show that Abraham's laugh was one of astonishment and not unbelief?

Sarah was later given the opportunity to hear for herself of the Lord's specific promise to her. Read verses 1–15 for that account. According to verse 12, what was Sarah's response?

In what ways was her response similar to, yet very different from, Abraham's?

Yes, Sarah was 90 years old. Yes, she had waited decades for the fulfillment of God's promise. The thought of bearing a child at this time in her life is beyond even the greatest level of faith! Yet, that apparently was no excuse. What was the Lord's response to Sarah? (vv. 13, 14)

Is *anything* too hard for the Lord? Have we ever the right to question His promises of provision, no matter how impossible they may seem?

Now read Genesis 21:1–13. How did the Lord fulfill His promise to Sarah? (vv. 1–7)

What situation arose between the offspring of Sarah and Hagar? (v. 9)

What was Sarah's response? (v. 10)

Why might this have been so distressing for Abraham? (v. 11)

Why do you think God needed to tell Abraham to listen to Sarah?

Read Genesis 21:14–21. Highlight what happened to Hagar.

What did she run out of? (v. 15)

What did God replace it with? (v. 19)

God so miraculously and beautifully met Hagar, this single mother, in her hour of need. He had spoken to her twice and given her promise of provision and success. She had every reason to have full faith in God and to live accordingly. But what did she do instead? (v. 21)

Though this was Hagar's native homeland, it was a place of idolatry and worldliness. Why do you think she would have chosen an Egyptian over a Hebrew?

What does this reveal to you about Hagar?

Now turn back in your Bible and read Genesis 2:18—3:24.

BEHIND THE SCENES

Eve was divine inspiration in every respect, fashioned in perfect form by the hand of God. God's ultimate gift to Adam was an enticing package, displaying beauty of form and grace in manner. Inwardly was sure to be found intelligence, humor, creativity, inspiration—an eternal gift that could be rediscovered again and again. Her environment was lovely, her relationship exciting, her every need was met, and all unimpaired by sin.

According to the first part of Genesis 3:2, what was Eve's first, and gravest mistake?

Compare 3:3 with 2:16, 17. How did Eve change God's directive for her and Adam?

What does God make clear about our changing His Word to suit our own desires? (Check Prov. 30:5, 6 and Rev. 22:18, 19.)

What tactic did Satan employ to tempt Eve to doubt God's Word? (v. 4)

When the Devil is not lying directly, he is often telling halftruths. How was this done in 3:5?

So we see that the enemy of our souls does not always tempt us with an obvious ploy that we would surely recognize and deny. Instead, he encourages us to speculate about what might be ours if we reach for things contrary to God's desire.

In verse 6, "the desire to become wise seemed quite reasonable to the woman. Unfortunately, her definition of wise was human self-rule, not God-dependency as taught in Proverbs 1:7."[3]

     WORD WEALTH

Understanding, *sachal* (sah-*chahl*). To be wise, behave wisely; to understand, be instructed; to wisely consider; to be prudent and intelligent. *Sachal* describes the complex, intelligent thinking process that occurs when one observes, ponders, reasons, learns, and reaches a conclusion.[4]

Now read Proverbs 1:7. "'The fear of the LORD': Expressed in many ways, this is the theme repeated throughout [Proverbs] as the key, the means, the secret of obtaining genuine wisdom. It is not the terror of a tyrant, but the kind of awe and respect which will lead to obedience to Him who is the wisest of all."[5]

What does Proverbs 1:7 show was lacking in Eve, as she chose to disobey God's command?

Was it probable that Eve was *intelligent*? Why?

Was Eve a *wise* woman? Explain.

How are wisdom and faith linked? (Proverbs 2:1–8 may help you form an answer.)

Why do you think Eve gave of the fruit to Adam? (Gen. 3:6)

Why do you think Adam partook with her, knowing full well it was wrong?

Adam blames Eve for their condition (v. 12). Whom does Eve blame? (v. 13)

What does God's Word say about laying blame and taking time to speculate about sin? Read James 1:14, 15 and copy it below. (It would be worth memorizing.)

Eve's downfall was not initially a case of blatant rebellion, but began when she doubted God's Word was true. Though she became "the first to violate the divine regulations governing their life (2:16, 17; 3:6), the Word of God holds Adam as the disobedient one, who knowingly broke trust with God (Rom. 5:12, 17; 1 Tim. 2:14). This fact does not intimate that the woman was less intelligent or more vulnerable to deception than the man, but that under the circumstances in which the Fall of man occurred, deception of the woman preceded active disobedience of the man."[6] Thus, it is clear that our lack of faith in God's Word can open wide the door to deception.

Now turn in your Bible to Genesis 24 and read the entire chapter. (Rebekah's being chosen as a bride for Isaac will be studied in more detail in a later lesson.) How did Isaac respond to Rebekah as his new bride?

Read Genesis 25:21. What was Isaac's petition of the Lord?

At a time when polygamy and concubines were common, why do you think Rebekah chose not to give one of her maids to Isaac?

What was the Lord's word to Rebekah about her pregnancy? (v. 23)

Now read Genesis 25:24–28. What problem was developing in the family of Isaac and Rebekah?

What continued division is reflected in 25:29–34?

Why do you think Esau showed so little respect for his birthright? (Note: "The birthright meant headship of the family and a double share of the inheritance [Deut. 21:17]."[7] Is there a possibility it was related to Rebekah's treatment of him?

What other incident showed Esau's lack of respect for his parents' opinions? (26:34, 35)

Now read Genesis 27:1–29. Apparently Isaac was not aware that Esau had sold Jacob his birthright. What did he ask Esau to do? (27:1–4)

Where was Rebekah while this was going on (v. 5), and why do you think she was there?

Summarize Rebekah's deceptive plan for Jacob (vv. 6–17).

Why do you think Jacob went along with something he knew was wrong?

Whom did Jacob use to further his selfish ambitions? (v. 20)

What was the result of Rebekah's plan? (vv. 18–29)

What additional problems developed because of the trickery? (v. 41)

Though the Word of the Lord to Rebekah (25:23) was fulfilled, what was actually lost by her attempts at performing it her own way? (27:42–44; 28:5)

How did Rebekah's actions display her lack of faith in God?

What was the future fruit of Rebekah's and Jacob's faithless deception? (Gen. 29:1–30)

BEHIND THE SCENES

In addition to Jacob's misery, Esau's marriage of rebellion and future children resulted in the race of the Edomites (Gen. 36:43), who were a source of torment to the Israelites for many years to come.

Eve, Sarah, and Rebekah suffered immeasurable losses because they doubted God's Word and relied upon their own wisdom (or lack thereof). And both Eve and Sarah influenced their husbands to participate in their faithless acts, the results of which humankind still bears.

But praise be to God, our All-Mighty Redeemer! "It is a remarkable token of divine grace that God, in His mercy and in His giving of the first promise of a Deliverer/Messiah (Gen. 3:15), chose to bring this about by Seed of the woman. In short, the one first scarred by sin is selected to be the one first promised to become an instrument of God's redemptive working."[8] And both Sarah and Rebekah were allowed the immense privilege of participation in the royal genealogy of the Lord Jesus Christ, not by what they earned or deserved, but by His marvelous grace and love.

  FAITH ALIVE

As you conclude the "Trial of Faith," summarize what you have learned about remaining faithful to God's Word when times of trial arise.

1. *Spirit-Filled Life Bible* (Nashville, TN: Thomas Nelson Publishers, 1991), 26, note on 15:2, 3.

2. Ibid.

3. Ibid., 8, note on 3:6.

4. Ibid., 1060, "Word Wealth: 3:15 understanding."

5. Ibid., 886, note on 1:7.

6. Ibid., 12, "Kingdom Dynamics: The First Woman: A Redemptive Instrument (Eve)."

7. Ibid., 42, note on 25:29–34.

8. Ibid., 12, "Kingdom Dynamics: The First Woman: A Redemptive Instrument (Eve)."

Lesson 4/Miriam— Daughter of Ministry

The Book of Micah illustrates the Lord's compassionate faithfulness and cites as an example His redemption of the children of Israel out of Egypt. In chapter 6 Micah refers to Moses, Aaron, and Miriam being sent before the people. The almost two million Israelites were led by this trio, one of whom was a woman. Miriam was allowed the privilege of great authority and responsibility in ministry, as we will discover.

But is that something now forbidden or discouraged for women? Are women in ministry living out of divine order? Does Scripture limit a woman's involvement in the church? Is a woman hindered due to her "spiritual inferiority" to a man? You may already have strong opinions on the subject, or you may never have addressed the issue at all. And though the Bible is neither contradictory nor vague on the subject, definitive conclusions are difficult to reach. But the question of women in church ministry involvement (especially in leadership roles) is valid, and deserves a thorough examination.

Open your Bible to Exodus 2, where Miriam is first mentioned (v. 4), though not by name. It is approximately 1526 B.C. and Pharaoh has commanded all newborn Israelite males to be killed.

Read Exodus 2:1–10. Miriam is only 7–12 years of age. What qualities for leadership does she already display?

Though we don't read specifically of Miriam again until Moses had led the Israelites from bondage in Egypt (Ex. 15), she was apparently already highly regarded among the people as a leader. Read Micah 6:4 and record the evidence of this.

Look at Exodus 15:20. What position of ministry did Miriam occupy?

BEHIND THE SCENES

A prophetess is one raised up by God and inspired by His Spirit to proclaim the will of God. The Hebrew word can also mean a singer of hymns, and, by association, the wife of a prophet. Although tradition holds that Miriam became the wife of Hur, who held up the hands of Moses, Scripture does not indicate by either word or influence this to be so. She apparently chose a life of singleness.

With her role as prophetess, what influence do you think Miriam had on Moses directly?

How might she have influenced the almost two million Israelite people?

BEHIND THE SCENES

Read Exodus 15:1–21.
Here we see Miriam, the first poetess in the Bible, in all her triumph. This Song of Deliverance is one of the earliest, and most inspiring, in Hebrew literature, though it's not clear what part, if any, Miriam composed. She is also the first woman singer recorded in Scripture.

How did Miriam use her gift of song to glorify the Lord? (vv. 20, 21)

Did she appear fearful of what others might think?

Given the dreary wilderness journey of the Israelites, what do you think Miriam's bold and cheerful gift of song ministered to the Israelites?

God allowed Miriam a position in ministry of great prominence and influence, rarely matched by other women in Israel's history. The Bible is faithful and complete and reflects the full character of the people it describes. Unfortunately, Miriam's life was not without blemish, as we will discover in the next lesson.

But for now, let us examine a woman's status and position before God as it relates to ministry. **How does God view women, and does He consider them secondary to men?**

 PROBING THE DEPTHS

If you want to examine the biblical grounds for balancing man's leadership role in comparison with woman's, a helpful resource may be found in *A Man's Starting Place,* by Jack W. Hayford, Regal Books, Ventura, CA.

Turn to Genesis 1, and read verse 27. It took the creation of both male and female to fully reflect the various attributes of God. What traits more common to women might reveal some of the character of God? (To get you started, look at Isaiah 49:14, 15 and 2 Corinthians 1:3, 4.)

Now read Genesis 1:28. What was God's original intent for both men and women?

How did a woman's appointed role change as a result of the Fall? (Gen. 3:16)

To whom was she now subject?

"The woman is not *directly* cursed, although it is obvious she comes under God's general curse. Rather, there will be a major marring of her appointed roles as wife and mother . . . . 'He shall rule over you' asserts the divine assignment of the husband's servant-leader role. There is no evidence that this was ever intended as a diminishing of the woman's person or giftedness, but rather as a redemptive role assigned the husband toward the wife as a means toward reinstating the original partnership."[1]

Did this divine directive of new order preclude God's ever speaking to or through a woman?

Read Genesis 21:9–21. Who is the distressed single mother, and what is her need?

What is God's personal response to her? (vv. 17–20)

Turn now to Judges and read 4:1—5:1. Though Deborah will be studied in depth later on, for now record the three distinct positions Deborah held.

Summarize how God used her on behalf of the children of Israel.

Now read 2 Kings 22:14–20. During the reign of King Josiah, the priests found the lost Book of the Law and discovered the nation had departed far from God. Who did

Hilkiah the high priest and Shaphan the scribe seek out for counsel and God's wisdom?

What do you think this infers about her reputation and influence as a servant of God?

Through Huldah's wise prophetic insight, Josiah repented, staying God's judgment. This led to one of the greatest revivals in history.

PROBING THE DEPTHS

For more on the sweeping reform that resulted from Huldah's allowing herself to be used as an instrument of God, read 2 Kings 23:1–27 and 2 Chronicles 34.

Though Queen Esther (Esth. 2—10) was without a specific title of "ministry," she was used profoundly of God for the salvation of the Jews and is certainly noteworthy (as will be discovered in a later lesson).

It is evident in the Old Testament, then, that God not only condoned, but blessed the sincere efforts of godly women in prominent spiritual leadership, and spoke to them and through them as well. By the time of Christ, the view of women had darkened considerably from what it was in Miriam's day. A popular Jewish saying was, "Thank God that I am neither a Gentile, a slave, nor a woman." It was taught that women were incapable of receiving religious instruction, and a rabbi could not speak openly to a woman in public, even if she was his wife or sister. But Jesus burst upon the scene, casting a bright new light on God's intended purpose for women in His kingdom.

Read John 11 and 12:1–11. (Notice in particular 11:5, 11.)

WORD WEALTH

Friend, *philos.* Compare "philosophy," "philology," "phil-harmonic." An adjective used as a noun, denoting a loved one, beloved, affectionate friend. The verb is *phileo,* which describes a love of emotion and friendship. *Philos* thus has a congeniality about it.[2]

At a time when friendships between men and women were disapproved of, what is Jesus' relationship not only with Lazarus, but with Mary and Martha?

Now read Luke 8:43–48. Keep in mind this woman has been considered unclean for twelve years. She is an outcast who is poor, weak, and afraid. How did Jesus respond to her?

Turn to John 20:15–18. Whom did Jesus trust with the vital first message of His resurrection?

From what you've seen thus far, comprise a list of words that would summarize Jesus' view and treatment of women during His earthly ministry (for example, compassionate, friendly).

Did Christ's death and resurrection limit or change a woman's spiritual status?

Turn to Galatians 3 and read verses 26–29. What are now the spiritual distinctions between men and women?

It is doubtful this means that in Christ, there is to be no structure or order. What, then, does it mean?

Now read Acts 1:13, 14. Who was present on the Day of Pentecost, when the Spirit was poured out? (v. 14)

Turn a bit further to Acts 2:14–21 and read Peter's quote from Joel 2. What spiritual status is given to women in this passage?

"The outpouring of the Spirit in the Old Testament had been largely reserved for the spiritual and national leaders of Israel. Under the New Covenant, however, the authority of the Spirit is for 'all flesh,' all who come under the New Covenant. Every believer is anointed to be a priest and king to God."[3]

Does it appear a woman's potential in ministry was diminished or increased by the death and resurrection of Jesus and the giving of the Holy Spirit? Explain.

It is safe to conclude, then, that a woman's freedom to minister is not restricted by God's view of her as a lesser creation, by any Old Testament precedent, or by some spiritual or other inherent limitation on her part.

What further light can be shed on the release of women in ministry through some examples from the New Testament?

Turn first to Luke 2:36–38. Anna's husband died after just seven years of marriage, and she dedicated the remainder of her life to service in the temple.

What did Anna realize about the child Jesus?

What did she do with that revelation?

Now read Romans 16:1, 2. "Paul calls [Phoebe] not only a servant of the church, but a helper of many. . . . Other versions translate the word 'servant' as 'deaconess.' Still others have called her 'minister'—inasmuch as in other scriptures where the Greek word *diakoneo* is used, it is translated 'minister.' According to many scholars it was Phoebe who carried the written book of Romans to the congregation."[4]

Now read Acts 18:2, 3, 18, 25, 26 and Romans 16:3–5. Write a brief description of the ministry of Priscilla. (It will also be useful when she is studied further in lesson 11.)

Look at Acts 21:8, 9 and note the ministry of Philip's four unmarried daughters.

"This reference to Philip's daughters' each exercising the gifts of prophecy makes clear that women did bring God's word by the power of the Holy Spirit and that such ministry was fully accepted in the early church."[5]

In the New Testament, then, women held a variety of offices. Summarize your own conclusions about these New Testament women and their ministries.

Evidently, women in both the Old and New Testament held important positions of ministry. But aren't there limitations and restrictions on women being used by God to minister? **Is age or experience a factor?**

Look first at 2 Kings 5:1–5, and list the main characters in the narrative.

From where was the young maid of Naaman's wife taken? (v. 2)

BEHIND THE SCENES

This girl was likely captured during a Syrian raid, and was placed in Naaman's home as a personal maid to his wife. She was just a teenager, but already well versed in the faith of her homeland. She knew her God, the Great Yahweh!

What was her bold observation to her mistress? (v. 3)

What was the outcome of her pointing the way for Naaman? (5:5–15)

What is the charge of 1 Timothy 4:12–16 regarding age and ministry?

Now turn again to Luke 2:36–38. How did Anna serve her God? (v. 37)

Anna found "favor in God's eyes, for He revealed the Messiah, the Hope of Israel, to her aged eyes. Her anointed ministry during later years of life holds forth a promise for older women. There is always ministry awaiting the sensitive, obedient, and pure—ministry that can influence and shape the rising generation."[6]

Also turn to and read Titus 2:3–5.

What have you observed from these examples about the limits of age and experience when it comes to a woman's being used of God?

What about marriage? Does it restrict the role a woman can fill in ministry?

Look again at Titus 2:4, 5. What does the Bible say are a married woman's priorities?

Now read Genesis 20:2–4. What is the only other thing that should come before a wife's husband and children?

Read 1 Corinthians 7:25–40, noting in particular verse 34. What is the married woman concerned with?

"Paul does not exalt the single state above the marriage state, but he does have a personal preference and urges all groups of the unmarried to consider the wisdom and spiritual benefits of a celibate life."[7]

Of what advantage does Paul speak when he encourages those who can to remain single?

A well-known Christian author, entertainer, and speaker (who was married with children) was asked how she dealt with the many demands on her time. Her reply was so simple, yet so immensely profound. She said, "Well, I have my devotions every day. I minister to God, and He gives to me. Out of that, I minister to the needs of my husband. Then I minister to my children by caring for their needs. And with whatever time I have left, I minister to the Body of Christ."

Look again at her response, but take out the marriage and children lines. How are the priorities affected?

What impact might the ages of a woman's children have on her ability to be released in ministry?

Is a husband's support for and agreement with his wife's ministry opportunities important? Read Ephesians 5:22–33. Husbands are to love their wives. What is the command to wives in verses 22, 24, and 33?

In 1 Timothy 3:8–12, Paul addresses the prerequisite for ministry of a properly ordered home. Who are included in his directives?

Not all the issues pertaining to women in ministry are as clear-cut as those addressed thus far. **What about the difficult passages of 1 Corinthians 14 and 1 Timothy 2?**
Read 1 Corinthians 14:26–40. Summarize the problems Paul was addressing in the church at Corinth.

It will aid our understanding of this passage to look at why Paul wrote this letter in the first place.

BEHIND THE SCENES

"Paul established the church at Corinth about A.D. 50–51. . . and continued to carry on correspondence and exercise care for the church after his departure. . . . The letter reveals some of the typical Greek cultural problems of Paul's day, including the gross sexual immorality of the city of Corinth. The Greeks were known for their idolatry, divisive philosophies, spirit of litigation, and rejection of the bodily resurrection. . . . The city was infamous for its sensuality and sacred prostitution. . . . The spirit of the city showed up in the church and explains the kind of problems the people faced."[8]

According to verse 40, what is the purpose of 1 Corinthians 14:26–40?

Look again at 14:34, 35 and summarize the directive.

According to verses 23–33, who else was asked to keep silent?

Now read 1 Corinthians 11:5, 6 in which Paul is also addressing order in the church.

BEHIND THE SCENES

"Uncovered hair or a shaved head could symbolize a loose or unclean condition (Lev. 14:8, 9; Num. 5:18)."[9] Also covered refers to her being "rightly related to her husband or other spiritual authority, a regulation incumbent upon *all* spiritual leaders—male or female."[10]

How do the directives of 1 Corinthians 11:5 and 14:34, 35 seem to conflict?

BEHIND THE SCENES

The speculation as to why Paul made the address of 14:34, 35 is vast. One view is that the women had been allocated to a separate court in the Jewish temples, so full participation in worship was a new experience. They were curious and asking questions during the meeting (v. 35). Another view is that Paul is addressing an issue of respect. The women, in their emancipated role, were taking issue with the men over what was being taught, and in doing so, were usurping authority and shaming their husbands in public. (Notice the Greek word for "woman" can also mean "wife.")

"The best interpretation is probably to see Paul as not forbidding women to manifest spiritual gifts in the service . . . . Rather, he prohibits undisciplined discussion that would disturb the service."[11]

In light of the whole of Scripture, summarize in your own words what you think 1 Corinthians 14:34, 35 means.

First Timothy 2:8–15 is the other difficult passage for women. Read that now and write down your observations or questions.

What is the first directive for women in this passage? (2:9, 10)

What does that tell you about the understanding of the women in Ephesus regarding right priorities and values?

What do the next two verses say? (vv. 11, 12)

Before studying verses 11 and 12, look at the following three verses (vv. 13–15). It is doubtful Paul meant women are more prone to deception, and therefore should not teach. Why, then, did he bring up Eve?

Turn in your Bible to Genesis 3, and read verse 16. To whom was Eve now subject because of the Fall?

Do you think her no longer sharing joint rule would be something she would miss or find difficult?

What, then, might Genesis 3:16 refer to when it says, "Your desire *shall be* for your husband"?

"Most likely the expression carries the idea that . . . she would desire to dominate her husband. . . . Note: the passage does not assert male dominance over females. It does assign husbandly responsibility for leadership in the marriage relationship."[12]

Do you think women ever need to be reminded of God's intended order of authority? (Eph. 5:22–24)

Do men ever need the same reminders? Look at 3 John 9, 10. What seemed to be the problem with Diotrephes?

Now look back at 1 Timothy 2:11, 12. In light of Paul's reference to Adam and Eve, to what might "have authority over a man" be referring?

Paul, in 1 Timothy 2:15, may have also been reminding women of their natural and primary function as childbearers, and that they should not look at any position in life, including church authority, as a higher priority or more desirable.

Finally, look again at 1 Timothy 2:12, "And I do not permit a woman to **teach**. . . ." Look up Titus 2:3, 4. How do these seem contradictory?

If a woman can teach, the qualification must appear further in 1 Timothy 2:12: "teach or have authority over a **man**. . . ." But turn to Acts 18:26. Who taught Apollos, the "eloquent man and mighty in the Scriptures" (v. 24) a more accurate way?

Because "teach" in this case carries with it the implications of doctrinal authority, verse 12 is most likely prohibiting a woman from taking "the authoritative office of apostolic teacher [of doctrine] in the church. It does not forbid women to educate, proclaim truth or exhort (prophesy)."[13]

What word (besides "women") is repeated in verses 11 and 12?

It is interesting to note that "silence" can be translated as "stillness, or keeping one's seat." In light of the study in 1 Corinthians 14:34, 35 and the problems in Ephesus, to what might these verses again be referring?

In conclusion, "though the place of men seems more pronounced in the number who filled leadership offices, there does not appear to be any direct restriction of privilege [for women in the Old or New Testament]. . . .

"The acceptance of women in a public place of ministry in the church is not a concession to the spirit of the feminist movement. But the refusal of such a place might be a concession to an order of male chauvinism, unwarranted by and unsupported in the Scriptures. Clearly, women did speak—preach and prophesy—in the early church."[14]

It is important to note that this study is not intended to provide reasons for women to either stay home and avoid ministry or leave home to pursue it. All aspects of our lives are subject to the fine scrutiny of Scripture to ensure our obedience to God's purpose at every season. Our pursuit of ministry, or any other goal, should not be based on personal ambition or desire, but subject to God's order for our lives, families, and His church.

1. *Spirit-Filled Life Bible* (Nashville, TN: Thomas Nelson Publishers, 1991), 9, note on 3:16.

2. Ibid., 1595, "Word Wealth: 11:11 friend."

3. Ibid., 1627, note on 2:17, 18.

4. Ibid., 1714, "Kingdom Dynamics: A Radiant Woman Minister (Phoebe)."

5. Ibid., 1668, "Kingdom Dynamics: Women and New Testament Ministry (Philip's Daughters)."

6. Ibid., 1512, "Kingdom Dynamics: An Effective Older Woman and Widow (Anna)."

7. Ibid., 1729, note on 7:25–40.

8. Ibid., 1717, 1718, "The Book of 1 Corinthians: Occasion and Date; Background."

9. Ibid., 1734, note on 11:5, 6.

10. Ibid., 1668, "Kingdom Dynamics: Women and New Testament Ministry (Philip's Daughters)."

11. Ibid., 1742, note on 14:34, 35.

12. Ibid., 9, note on 3:16.

13. Ibid., 1843, note on 2:11, 12.

14. Ibid., 1668, "Kingdom Dynamics: Women and New Testament Ministry (Philip's Daughters)."

Lesson 5/ Miriam— Daughter Who Spoke

Miriam was truly anointed and gifted of God as a ministering woman. She was a strong worship leader and a prophetess (Ex. 15:20, 21), fiercely loyal, and extremely patriotic to the cause of the Israelite nation.

Interestingly, the giftings of God can often seem like a "two-edged sword." Those areas where one is most gifted can at the same time be areas in which one is most prone to failure. We see one of the clearest instances of this in the life of Miriam. She was a gifted leader and spokesperson, but she began to think that she was qualified for more authority than God had apportioned for her. Unfortunately, she did more than think it; she spoke.

Turn to Numbers 12:1–5 and read the account of Miriam's failure. According to verse 1, what did Miriam and Aaron do?

Do you think the order of their names in the text had any significance? If so, what might that be?

What was the reason for their criticism of Moses? (v. 1)

 BEHIND THE SCENES

It is doubtful that Miriam and Aaron were criticizing Moses' wife because of her race as an Ethiopian, but more likely because she was not one of the people of the covenant. We do see precedent for this in other places in Scripture. In Genesis 24:37, Abraham is specific in his request that Isaac not take a bride from the Canaanites. Also, in Exodus 34:10–16, it is clear that the Israelites were not to covenant with idolatrous peoples, for fear that they themselves would become participants. The Ethiopians (Cushites) were a heathen and idolatrous nation.

Though Miriam and Aaron's complaint against Moses seemed legitimate, do you think the wife of Moses was really the issue? Explain.

In Numbers 12:2, how did they justify their criticism?

Look now at Genesis 3:1. What phrase from that verse is repeated in a similar fashion in Numbers 12:2?

Miriam and Aaron were questioning the validity of Moses as God's spokesperson, in order to discredit his authority and legitimize their complaint. If this were carried to its logical conclusion, whose word was actually being challenged?

The narrative includes that "Moses *was* very humble" (v. 3). Turn back in your Bible to Exodus 4 and read verses 1 and 10. What do these references imply about Moses?

Do you think Moses ever would have confronted Miriam and Aaron or dismissed their charges as insignificant? Why or why not?

How might Miriam and Aaron's criticism have affected Moses' ability to lead?

As leaders, how might their comments have affected the people?

According to Hebrews 12:14, 15, what was another of the potential dangers?

Read Numbers 12:4. STOP where you are and take a few minutes to imagine the situation. There were likely numerous possibilities running through Miriam's mind as to why God was summoning the trio. Pretend you are Miriam. What might some of your thoughts be at this point?

Now look at 12:5. It appears the possibilities for God's summons are narrowing. As Miriam, what would you be thinking *now*?

(You may now be yourself, and breathe a huge sigh of relief!)

In 12:6–8, the Lord asserts that "Yahweh's revelation to Moses is unique. It is direct ('plainly') and immediate ('face to face'); the prophets' revelations are in mediated forms. The clear lesson is that even prophets cannot presume to claim that their message is equal to that of Moses."[1]

Of the many things the Lord could have addressed, what did He ask Miriam and Aaron? (v. 8) Record His question below.

What do you think He meant?

What was the effect of Miriam and Aaron's actions upon God? (v. 9)

What was the instantaneous judgment upon Miriam? (v. 10)

Turn to Exodus 15:20, 21 and compare Miriam's condition then to her state in Numbers 12:10.

How was Miriam spared a certain and humiliating death? (Num. 12:11–14)

BEHIND THE SCENES

"'Seven days': This is the length of elapsed time prescribed for the priest's first and second inspections of leprosy (Lev. 13). The implication is that she was healed in response to Moses' prayer and would be pronounced clean after seven days. For spitting in the face as a sign of contempt, see Deuteronomy 25:9."[2]

Both Moses and Miriam desired the change of a situation, but went about it in different ways. Compare Moses' actions of 12:13 with Miriam's actions of 12:1, 2. What were the differences?

It is said, "A situation does not make the person; it reveals the person." What was revealed about Miriam?

What does the Bible say our words reveal? (Matt. 12:34)

According to Proverbs 27:19, what does the heart reveal?

What else does Proverbs tell us about our words? Look at 18:21. **What does this verse really mean? How do our words have power?**

Turn in your Bible to Genesis 1. Read verses 3, 6, 9, 11, 14, 20, 24, and 26. What phrase is repeated at the beginning of each of these verses?

According to these references, how was the world, and all it contains, created?

How is it now held together? (Heb. 1:3)

So God is a creative being, who made and upholds all things by the power of His Word. In whose image were we created? (Gen. 1:27)

 BEHIND THE SCENES

"Man is distinct from the rest of creation. The Divine Tri-une Counsel determined that man was to have God's image and likeness. Man is a spiritual being who is not only body, but also soul and spirit. He is a moral being whose intelligence, perception, and self-determination far exceed that of any other earthly being."[3]

As an example, what is one aspect of the creative power given to a man and woman? (Gen. 1:28; 4:1)

Now turn to John 1:1. What was from "the beginning"?

 BEHIND THE SCENES

"'The Word' is Jesus Christ, the eternal, ultimate expression of God. In the Old Testament God spoke the world into existence; in the gospel God spoke His final word through the living Word, His Son. The phrase 'the Word was

God' attributes deity to the Word without defining all of the
Godhead as 'the Word.'"[4]

What additional power (authority) was given to the saints
by the Word, Jesus Christ, through His sacrifice and through
His name? Read John 14:12–14 and Luke 10:17.

BEHIND THE SCENES

Now read Matthew 16:19.
"'Keys' denote authority. Through Peter, a representative
of the church throughout the ages, Jesus is passing on to His
church His authority or control to 'bind' and to 'loose on the
earth.' The Greek construction behind 'will be bound' and 'will
be loosed' indicates that Jesus is the One who has activated
the provisions through His Cross; the church is then charged
with implementation of what He has released through His life,
death, and resurrection. . . . Binding and loosing have to do
with forbidding or permitting. . . . For example, if someone is
bound by sin, the church can 'loose' him by preaching the provision of freedom from sin in Jesus Christ (Rom. 6:14). If
someone is indwelt by a demon, the church can 'bind' the
demon by commanding its departure (Acts 16:18)."[5]

What power is given when we abide in Him and His
Word abides in us? (John 15:7)

WORD WEALTH

Abide, *meno.* To stay (as in a given place of expectancy),
continue, dwell, endure, be present, remain, stand, tarry.

Use the meanings of the Greek word for *abide* (from the Word
Wealth above), and write a definition of what it means to
"abide in Him."

When is God's Word abiding in us? (John 5:38)

What dimension was added to the power of our words through the giving of the Holy Spirit? (Acts 1:8; 10:44)

Look back over this lesson thus far, and write a summary of why your words have power.

God has given us, His unique creation, the gift and power of speech. "Capacity and ability constitute accountability and responsibility. We should never be pleased to dwell on a level of existence lower than that on which God has made it possible for us to dwell. We should strive to be the best we can be and to reach the highest levels we can reach. To do less is to be unfaithful stewards of the life [and gift] entrusted to us."[6]

How, then, can we be faithful stewards of the gift entrusted to us: our speech?

Turn to James 3:1–12. It is obvious James had strong feelings about the power of the tongue! It is true "'the tongue is a little member' (v. 5), but its power and influence for good or bad are out of proportion to its size."[7]

In 2 Corinthians 2:11, the Bible warns that we should not be ignorant of Satan's devices, lest he take advantage of (use) us. Through the spoken word, Miriam became a tool in the enemy's hand to try and destroy one of God's chosen leaders. (For further reading, see the story of how Potiphar's wife was similarly used against Joseph in Genesis 39.)

Look again at Numbers 12:1, 2. Do you think Miriam and Aaron's words against Moses just simultaneously "popped out," without any previous thought or discussion? What must have taken place before this incident?

The Bible aptly calls this type of discussion "whispering." Depending upon your translation, it is also called "gossip," "talebearing," "slander," or "evil speaking" (among others). It has been appropriately defined as "saying something you like about someone you don't," and can produce life-extinguishing consequences.

KINGDOM EXTRA

There are innumerable scripture references that reveal the dangers and problems stemming from this kind of talk, as well as the life-begetting power in the tongue. A good place to gain further insight is in the Book of Proverbs. You might want to read one chapter a day for the next month and underline each verse that relates to the tongue, the heart, or the words of the mouth.

Now look at James 3:8. From this verse, it appears the tongue is not tamable. But is it possible to "bridle the tongue"? to control what we say with our mouths and how we say it? James doesn't lay out much hope.

However, the Bible never tells us to do anything that the Lord does not give us the strength to accomplish (1 Cor. 10:13; Phil. 4:13). Even James concedes "these things ought not to be so" (3:10); therefore, it must be possible, by God's grace, to tame the tongue.

First, look at Ephesians 4:17, 22–24. When we become new creatures in Christ, summarize what should change.

List the ways we are to "put off the old man" through our words (Eph. 4:25, 29, 31; 5:4).

Now list the ways we are to "put on the new man" in regard to our speech (Eph. 4:23, 25, 29, 32; 5:19, 20).

What does Proverbs 16:23 say a wise-hearted person can do?

Apparently, we are able to control what we say. But why, then, is our tongue such a stumbling block? (James 3:2) You will recall that Matthew 12:34 says, "Out of the abundance of the heart the mouth speaks." *Therefore, problems with the mouth are directly related to the problems of the heart—a heart in need of transformation.*

Read Romans 12:1, 2. What are we to present to God?

What does Paul tell us in these verses not to do?

Conforming to the standards of this world is destructive to our minds (heart).

 WORD WEALTH

Conformed, *suschematizo.* Compare "scheme" and "schematic." Refers to conforming oneself to the outer fashion or outward appearance, accommodating oneself to a model or pattern. *Suschematizo* occurs elsewhere in the New Testament only in 1 Peter 1:14, where it describes those conforming themselves to worldly lusts. Even apparent or superficial conformity to the present world system or any accommodation to its ways would be fatal to the Christian life.[8]

If we are not to conform to this world, what **are** we to do? (Rom. 12:2)

How is this accomplished? Look first at Romans 10:17. What role does God's Word have in the renewing of our minds (heart)?

Now look at Ephesians 5:26. What can be accomplished through the Word?

Read Hebrews 4:12. Write down what the Word is and what it does.

According to Romans 15:4, what else is given by God's Word?

"The Word of God illuminated by the Holy Spirit is the only true means for transforming the human heart. Salvation by faith is a specific occasion, while the renewing of the mind by the Word is a continuing process. The disciple devotes himself to God's Word to be transformed into a holy person, radiantly Christ-like and radically different from the world. Spiritual disciples devour God's Word because in it is the key to a more dynamic relationship with their living Lord and a greater availability to the Holy Spirit."[9]

FAITH ALIVE

Did you know you are right now in the process of transformation? As you are reading and studying God's Word, He is revealing to you the intentions of your heart (Heb. 4:12). As you submit those intentions to His lordship and commit yourself to His ways, your heart will become more like His. Look up Proverbs 16:3 and write it below.

God renews the mind (heart) through His Word. How can one keep his or her mind from being "repolluted" by the things of the world? Look up Philippians 4:6–8, and read it several times.

According to this passage, what are we to be anxious about? (v. 6)

What should be done instead? (v. 6)

We have the promise of God's peace, regardless of what circumstances tell us ("surpasses all understanding"), if we meet the above conditions. What will this peace do? (Phil. 4:7)

 ## WORD WEALTH

Guard (kept), *phroureo.* A military term picturing a sentry standing guard as protection against the enemy. We are in spiritual combat, but God's power and peace are our sentinels and protectors.[10]

Did you know this was also the cure for depression (which can also assail our mind and heart)? Look at Proverbs 12:25. Beneath all the overwhelming layers of emotion related to depression, what is the actual cause?

Turn back again to Philippians 4:6. What are we to do with our anxieties (fears, worries, doubts)?

What will then replace your depression? (4:7)

The mind (heart) can become distracted by so many things. Read Luke 12:22–32. What does Jesus ask in verse 26?

What does He say we are not to have? (v. 29)

Worry over temporal things can be overwhelming. What puts those desires in their proper priority? (v. 31)

What is the ironic result? (v. 31)

The mind (heart) can also act as a battleground. Turn to 2 Corinthians 10:4, 5. What are we able to do with the thoughts that war in our minds against the truths of God?

"Here Paul refers specifically to warfare in the mind, against arrogant, rebellious ideas and attitudes (which he terms 'arguments'), and against 'every high thing' (pride) opposed to the true 'knowledge of God'. The aim is to bring 'every' disobedient 'thought into . . . obedience' to Christ."[11]

Once our thoughts are under captive obedience, what then? Turn to Philippians 4:8, 9 and read it once again. Write the seven key words that convey the things we *are* to think about.

"Character and conduct begin in the mind. Our actions are affected by the things we dwell on in our thoughts. Paul cautions to concentrate on things that will result in right living and in God's peace."[12]

Choose at least two things from Philippians 4:8 that you know you need to spend more time "meditating on."

It is important to remember that the transforming of your mind is a continual process, not a one-time occurrence. It requires the *daily* maintenance of bringing your petitions to God and feeding upon His Word. Remain faithful, and you'll be amazed by the progress!

1. *Spirit-Filled Life Bible* (Nashville, TN: Thomas Nelson Publishers, 1991), 211, note on 12:4–8.

2. Ibid., 211, note on 12:14.

3. Ibid., 6, "Kingdom Dynamics: Man's Intrinsic Value."

4. Ibid., 1573, note on 1:1.

5. Ibid., 1436, note on 16:19.

6. Ibid., 6, "Kingdom Dynamics: Man's Intrinsic Value."

7. Ibid., 1898, note on 3:2–12.

8. Ibid., 1707, "Word Wealth: 12:2 conformed."

9. Ibid., 1716, "Truth-in-Action through Romans."

10. Ibid., 1907, "Word Wealth: 1:5 kept."

11. Ibid., 1763, note on 10:4, 5.

12. Ibid., 1806, note on 4:8.

Lesson 6/Deborah— Daughter of Wise Leadership

Leadership is not a responsibility afforded to only a few but a privilege given by God to all. For leading is simply guiding or influencing the way of another. And Jesus asked every believer to participate in showing others the way to eternal life (Acts 1:8).

So whether it is across the sea or across the street, as a state senator or a team mom, as a corporate executive or a PTA committee member, we have all been given the opportunity to lead and influence others, and to help them find their way to The Way, Jesus Christ.

Open your Bible to Judges and read chapters 4 and 5. As you familiarize yourself with the account of Deborah, make note of the main characters, the responsibilities they carried, and any questions you have.

 ## BEHIND THE SCENES

"The Book of Judges covers a chaotic period in Israel's history from about 1380 to 1050 B.C. Under the leadership of Joshua, Israel had generally conquered and occupied the land of Canaan, but large areas remained yet to be possessed by the individual tribes. Israel did evil in the sight of the Lord continually and *'there was* no king in Israel; everyone did *what was* right in his own eyes' (21:25). By deliberately serving foreign gods, the people of Israel broke their covenant with the Lord. As a result, the Lord delivered them into the hands of various oppressors. Each time the people cried out to the Lord, He faithfully raised up a judge to bring deliverance to His people. These judges whom the Lord chose and anointed with His Spirit were military and civil leaders."[1] As this scene opens, Israel has been oppressed for twenty years by the Canaanites under Jabin. Deborah is the current judge God has set over Israel.

We will see in the life of Deborah seven basic qualities of leadership that allowed God to use her more effectively. We begin our study with the first of those.

THE CALL

In Judges 4:4, we are first introduced to Deborah by her name (which means "Honeybee"). What three specific roles that Deborah filled are mentioned in this verse?

Deborah had a definite calling from God, and He raised her up and enabled her to fulfill that call as she responded to His will. God has also called each one of us to lead, through whatever sphere of influence we're afforded.

Turn in your Bible to 2 Timothy 1:8, 9. According to verse 9, what two things has God done for us?

What qualifies us for His calling? (v. 9)

In the New King James translation, this passage begins with, "Therefore do not be ashamed . . . ." Because few of us will sit as a judge over a nation, we may feel we are not called or that we are insignificant in God's kingdom. But it is clear you *are* called by Him for a purpose and should never feel ashamed of your role.

Now turn to 1 Corinthians 1:26–29. If we are ever tempted to think we don't have what it takes to be called by God, what does this verse tell us to the contrary?

All believers are called by God and chosen for His purpose. And He needs each one of us in order to complete His will. Read 1 Corinthians 12:12. Of what is the body comprised?

"Each member of the [human] body relates to and depends upon other parts of the body. Each contributes to the welfare of the entire body. So are all believers as members of the body of Christ. . . . There is no Christian brother [or sister] whom we do not need."[2]

So, with or without an official title, all are called to contribute to Christ's body, His church; and lead by the example of our lives (Phil. 4:9). But that demands another attribute necessary for good leadership . . .

THE COMMITMENT

In Judges 4:4 Deborah is called a prophetess, as was Miriam (Ex. 15:20). She was also a judge, a recognized office of both national and spiritual leadership. This required her to render decisions on peoples' inquiries at a time when they sought reasons for their oppression (4:3).

Deborah's ability to discern the mind and purposes of God was not something she could have acquired overnight. What kind of things do you think Deborah did as a young woman to become so wise?

What did Jesus say about that kind of commitment? Turn to Matthew 25:21 and record His words.

Deborah's commitment was built on a solid foundation and only grew stronger. According to Judges 4:5, what would she do daily?

In light of the condition of the children of Israel (4:1) and the things they must have asked her about (4:3), do you think her role was pleasant or easy? Explain.

Why would that kind of leadership require commitment?

Deborah was committed to the ways of the Lord, the people of the Lord, and, most importantly, to the Person of the Lord God. Turn to 2 Chronicles 16:9. According to the first portion of that verse, what did God see in Deborah that allowed Him to use her?

Though some Bible versions read "whose heart is perfect," it is best translated as "loyal." Look up the word "loyal" in the dictionary, and write the definition that best suits Deborah.

Deborah was a called and committed leader, but neither of those came without a willingness to embrace . . .

THE COST

Deborah was effective as a leader, but it was not without cost. She had to be uncompromisingly loyal and faithful to God, even while those around her were not.

Turn to Judges 2 and read verses 11–23. What were some of the "evils" (4:1) in which the children of Israel were participating?

Do you think Deborah was ever tempted to compromise herself and participate? Why or why not?

What might the personal costs have been to Deborah in order to lead as she did? (4:5, 8–10) (Consider her marriage, her time, the culture, and so on.)

Deborah was obviously a gifted and talented leader. Could she have used her abilities for personal gain? Explain.

Now look at Philippians 3:7–11. What was Paul willing to trade "for the excellence of the knowledge of Christ"?

What did he receive in return? (3:10)

Though serving God by leading others has its costs, it also has benefits that far outweigh any loss we may incur (2 Cor. 4:16–18). What might some of those benefits be?

 FAITH ALIVE

If the Lord were to impress upon you today His desire for you to take on a new role of leadership, what are at least two things you'd be willing to lose (give up) in order to free up that time (for example, two hours of your free time or a hobby)?

But doesn't leading require certain skills? In a matter of speaking, yes. Deborah's life shows us how to have . . .

THE CAPACITY

Read Judges 4:6, 7. What qualities necessary for effective leadership do you think Deborah displayed?

What other creative abilities did she possess? (5:1)

Is that why God was able to use her? Or did we just learn that God can use anyone, regardless of skill? (1 Cor. 1:26–29) Yes, we did. And that's true, He can. (Consider Balaam's donkey in Numbers 22:22–30.)

But God also gifts each one of us with talents and abilities that He desires to infuse with His life and multiply for His glory. Turn to Romans 12:6–8. List at least three gifts Paul exhorts believers to use.

Now turn to 1 Corinthians 12:8–11. List three more ways God works through His saints.

Now turn to Ephesians 4:11 and choose three more offices through which God edifies His body.

This is just a sampling of the many ways God gifts His people for the blessing of His church; and it does not even include the many talents and abilities He bestows as well.

Using these capacities to influence people for our own gain is called "earthly" wisdom (James 3:14, 15). Using them for God's purposes is "wisdom from above" (James 4:17). But how do we receive the kind of wisdom that allows our gifts to become effective for His sake?

First read Proverbs 9:10. Where does wisdom begin?

This is not a fear as in terror; but one of awe or reverence, that involves "reproofs, instruction, advice and humility."[3] How does one receive this type of instructive wisdom from God? Turn to James 1:5 for the simple, yet profound, answer and write it below.

According to James 1:5, to whom will God give wisdom? And how will He give it?

 WORD WEALTH

Wisdom, *sophia.* Practical wisdom, prudence, skill, comprehensive insight, Christian enlightenment, a right application of knowledge, insight into the true nature of things.[4]

Jesus, in Matthew 12:42, spoke of a wise queen who understood the value of God's wisdom and the importance of seeking it out. (You can learn more about her in 1 Kin. 10:1–13.)

The wisdom of God is essential for fruitful leadership and is certainly worthy of seeking. What does the Bible promise to those who seek it? (Prov. 8:17; Matt. 7:7, 8; Heb. 11:6)

What should be desired beyond wisdom? (Prov. 4:7)

By what means can we obtain it? (Prov. 9:10)

"Wisdom is knowing the truth and how to apply it. . . . Understanding is knowledge seasoned and modified by wisdom and insight."[5] Both come from knowing God; that is also how we gain . . .

THE CONFIDENCE

Read Judges 4:6, 7. Did Deborah seem confident in her address of Barak? Why or why not?

How did she sound later in verses 9 and 14?

What was the effect both times on Barak? (vv. 10, 14)

Deborah was fully convinced the Israelites would have the victory. From whom did she receive such bold counsel? (v. 6)

According to Deborah, how would their success be given? (vv. 7, 14)

Deborah's faith in God and confidence of His purpose was unswerving. How does Judges 4:8 show us her faith was evident to others?

On whom did Deborah depend at every turn? (vv. 9, 14)

Though Deborah was a bold and confident leader, it was not born out of her great abilities or natural wisdom. It stemmed from her relationship with God and what she knew He was capable of doing through a willing vessel. She was no doubt aware of the mighty exploits of those God had used before her, including Moses and Joshua, and her confidence showed she believed all she had heard about the great Yahweh. She knew Him to be faithful and true to His people—enough so for her to act upon it. How is that seen in Judges 4:9, 10?

What does Daniel 11:32 confirm about those who know their God?

Deborah's confidence and strength was admirably balanced with a receptive humility, totally void of arrogance or pride. (Another example of such balance is found in Numbers 27. Turn there and read verses 1–11 for the story of the daughters of Zelophehad.)

Another leadership-enhancing quality found in Deborah was . . .

THE COURAGE

According to Judges 4:3, what were Deborah and her people up against in opposing Sisera?

Along with that advantage, Sisera commanded as many as 100,000 troops. How many did Barak deploy? (4:10)

Read Judges 4:6–10. What willing act by Deborah showed immense courage on her part?

It was a brave heart that was willing to initiate action against the forces opposed to God's purposes for His people. But Deborah knew the Spirit behind their mission was far greater than any opposition they could face. She already understood the principles later revealed by God through His Word. (See, for example, 1 Sam. 17:47; Is. 54:17; 2 Cor. 10:3–5.)

Though Deborah led the people in an actual battle, she had the courage to believe God would deliver the enemy into their hands, as He had promised.

FAITH ALIVE

Is there a point in your own life where a battle is raging? Is there a strategy of the enemy operating in opposition to the purpose and will of God for you? Take courage, dear one. The Lord is on your side. He is willing and able to deliver. You are *more* than a conqueror in Christ (Rom. 8:37–39). Choose to align yourself with Him, according to the provisions of His Word (Deut. 7:1–26). Then take the authority He has given you in prayer, resist the enemy by renouncing his works, and watch him flee (James 4:7).

Deborah exhibited confidence and courage, born out of her commitment to God. She was a woman who had . . .

THE CONVICTION

Read Judges 4:14. Deborah was absolutely **convinced** God would deliver them. Regardless of the impossible circumstances, she trusted enough in God's Word to *act*. In 4:9, Deborah talked to Barak. What five words followed their conversation?

Deborah stood against fear and complacency and rose beyond her natural inclinations. She was so convinced of God's faithfulness, she was willing to put herself on the line for it (4:9). And her conviction was contagious. How did Barak and his soldiers respond in Judges 4:14?

Her desire to see God's people set free stirred within them the courage to want to free themselves.

What was the final result of Barak and Deborah's courageous campaign against Sisera? (4:15, 16)

PROBING THE DEPTHS

For a clearer picture of the battle itself, read Judges 5, Deborah's Song of Victory.

Sisera was the only Canaanite to escape plunder by the Israelites. But what was his rather gruesome fate? (4:17–24)

Jael, too, showed great conviction. She would have been highly rewarded for assisting the Canaanite commander, but instead chose to act on behalf of the Israelite nation. Her loyalty was praised by Deborah (Judg. 5:24). This rather shocking incident seems foreign to our understanding, but to a people in the midst of war, radical action was sometimes necessary. The results of Deborah's skilled and anointed leadership is probably best summarized in Judges 5:31: "So the land had rest for forty years."

To secure in your understanding the seven qualities of leadership Deborah exhibited, review this lesson and consider each point, particularly as it relates to every believer who is willing to be led by God and to lead others for His glory.

1. *Spirit-Filled Life Bible* (Nashville, TN, Thomas Nelson Publishers, 1991), 343, "The Book of Judges: Background."
2. Ibid., 1737, "Kingdom Dynamics: All Believers Are Members of the Body of Christ."
3. Ibid., 925, "Truth-in-Action through Proverbs."
4. Ibid., 1636, "Word Wealth: 6:10 wisdom."
5. Ibid., 925, "Truth-in-Action through Proverbs."

Lesson 7/Ruth—Daughter of Faithfulness

As daughters of the Almighty God, we desire with all our hearts to serve Him. Yet we may feel limited by our situations in life, thinking all the really great and important things are being done by others, and that we have somehow been relegated to the eternally mundane. But only God knows the importance of the small "dailies."

It was Jesus Himself who spent many years toiling faithfully in a carpenter's shop; and it was also Jesus who reminded us on three separate occasions about our faithfulness in the small things being the key to release of bigger things (Matt. 25:21; Luke 16:10; 19:17). In this lesson, we will examine the life of a woman who displayed great faithfulness in spite of difficult circumstances, and how that allowed the sovereign hand of God to move on her behalf.

Begin the study by reading all four chapters of Ruth. Write down any questions, principles, or comments you'd like to record.

Now look at Ruth 1:1, 2. List the initial characters in the story of Ruth and describe their relationship to each other.

 KINGDOM EXTRA

You can answer further background and cultural questions related to the Book of Ruth by consulting study Bibles, reference books, or Bible concordances and encyclopedias. One place to begin might be with the Moabites (Ruth's heritage).

BEHIND THE SCENES

The Book of Ruth opens somewhere between 1150 and 1100 B.C., during the period of the Judges. Turn to Judges 2 and 3 and read of the conditions of the Israelites during this period of history.

In Ruth 1:1–5, we read of a famine that caused Elimelech and his family to depart Judah and move to Moab.

BEHIND THE SCENES

"The famine (1:1) was the natural by-product of sin, a judgment imposed by the people upon themselves through their disobedience. The Lord had previously warned that the land itself would turn against them if they were unfaithful to Him (Deut. 28:15, 16, 23, 24, 38–40). Further, Elimelech's choice to move his family to the country of Moab (1:2) is not evidenced as being God's direction but simply his own decision."[1]

Did this land prove to be a haven from difficulty? What was this place of Ruth's origin actually like? To find out, first read Genesis 19:30–37. We discover in verse 37 that the origins of Moab were unrighteous at best!

PROBING THE DEPTHS

For more on the history of Moab and Israel, read Numbers 22—31.

Look now at Deuteronomy 23:3, 4. Why had Moab been excluded from the congregation?

Ruth's background is repeatedly stressed throughout her story, and we will study its significance in the next lesson. But with the cursed heritage of a godless, idolatrous people, how would you explain Ruth's sensitivity to the things of God? From whom might she have heard of the God of Israel? (You may want to complete this answer after further study.)

What does this tell you about companionship's power?

PROBING THE DEPTHS

> For more on what Scripture reveals about the influence we can have on our families and others (or vice versa), read Proverbs 22:24, 25; 1 Timothy 4:12; Titus 2:7, 8; 1 Peter 2:11–25 and 3:1, 2.

So we have learned that Moab was not the haven Elimelech's family had hoped it would be. Though Naomi's sons found wives there, both Ruth and Naomi experienced much pain and loss.

We read how Naomi feels "the hand of the LORD has gone out against me" (Ruth 1:13). "Naomi's perspective is understandable, given the limited revelation of God's true nature at the time (1 Sam. 3:1). However, her reaction should not be construed as a commentary either on the nature of God or on the actual cause of her condition."[2]

Though Naomi thought God had turned against her, let's look at some of the circumstances that actually led to her discouraged and embittered state.

First read Judges 6:1–10 and list some of the difficulties Naomi may have experienced both in Judah and when departing for Moab.

Once Naomi arrived in Moab, the heartache continued. Read Ruth 1:3 and record Naomi's first loss.

Now read Ruth 1:4. Though Naomi's sons found wives, there is no mention of their having children. Why might this have been difficult for both Ruth and Naomi? (For additional help, read Deut. 28:1–4, 15–18.)

Ruth 1:5 tells us of Ruth and Naomi's further heartbreak. What happened?

Read Ruth 1:6–9. Naomi had lost almost all of what was precious to her and had decided to leave Moab and return to the land of Judah, where her God was worshiped and where she likely had many friends. But she had decided first to release her daughters-in-law to remain in Moab, the land of their birth. What are some reasons why Naomi would have desired to release her daughters-in-law?

Why might it have been better for her to keep them with her?

Ruth and Orpah decided to continue with Naomi (1:10–14). Yet, out of her concern, Naomi again entreated them to stay on in Moab. In verses 11–13, you can feel Naomi's helpless despair at having very little left to offer, as well as her confusion about God's hand in her life.

 KINGDOM EXTRA

Ruth 1:11–13 refers to the custom of the Levirate marriage. More can be found in Genesis 38:11, Deuteronomy 25:5–10, and Matthew 22:24.

Now read Ruth 1:15–18. Finally, through tears, Orpah conceded to her mother-in-law's wishes and returned to Moab. Yet, "Ruth is insistent, 'Entreat me not to leave you.' Her oft-quoted poem of commitment is not mere emotion. She clearly is reaching beyond friendship to faith. 'The Lord do so' indicates Ruth understands the nature of Yahweh. She invokes His name with an oath. Her commitment is rooted in an understanding of the living God, of whom she has [primarily] learned from Naomi."[3]

 KINGDOM EXTRA

Check a reference book that includes manners or customs of Bible times to find out more about the methods and conditions of travel.

Look up the word "loyalty" in the dictionary and write the definition that best describes Ruth.

Loyalty is a concept that seems so foreign to today's culture. Why do you think that is so?

Ruth would likely face prejudice in Judah as a Moabitess and might never remarry for the same reason. Take a moment and consider the other things Ruth stood to lose or had to let go of to remain loyal to Naomi and faithful to what she felt was right. (Ruth 2:11 will get you started.) Record your thoughts below.

It was at this point that Ruth had to make a conscious, willful (v. 18, "determined," or "steadfastly minded"[4]) decision about her future. She could have remained in a place of comfort and familiarity, but she was unwilling to compromise her loyalty to Naomi or her faith in God. So, refusing to allow fear to rule her, she pressed ahead into the new place God had for her. We will later look at what happened as a result of Ruth's decision.

Now read Luke 9:62. These can sound like harsh words, until one realizes "that service for His enterprise demands undivided attention. 'Is [not] fit for the kingdom of God' means that halfhearted discipleship eliminates one from God's maximum use."[5]

Turn to Philippians 3 and read verses 12–15. Write out verse 13.

 FAITH ALIVE

Pause to reflect and prayerfully allow the Holy Spirit to reveal any areas in your life where He would desire to "move you on." What would He ask you to leave behind or let go of from your past in order to reach unhindered toward His fullest purposes ahead? Where would the Lord desire to bring for-giveness or redemption in order to free you to embrace fully His complete plan? It is easy to get caught in the mire of "what if I'd done this, not gone there, or developed this tal-ent?" But remember that the Lord forgives you and your past when you give it to Him (1 John 1:9). He doesn't even remember it anymore (Jer. 31:34)—why should you? Write down what the Holy Spirit is showing you about moving for-ward in your life.

In Ruth 1:19–22, we read of Ruth and Naomi's return to Bethlehem. It is clear that Naomi was still struggling and con-fused in her view of God. She "reflects human nature in gen-eral as she blames God, rather than personal choices and sin nature, for the destructive and painful things she is experienc-ing. Naomi's behavior is characteristic of a person outside the covenant; thus she inappropriately indicates her circumstance to be the result of God's punitive action."[6]

Though it would appear Naomi was justified in her feelings due to the difficulty of her circumstances, it is important to note that she made a *willful choice* in how she would respond to God in the midst of her trial.

What do you think Ruth thought of Naomi's response?

Though having experienced much of the same loss, how does it appear Ruth responded?

As we begin in chapter 2, we see Ruth as a woman of action. In considering her plight with Naomi, who was too old to work, Ruth again made the decision to lay down her own comforts and desires to do what needed to be done. Read all of chapter 2, noting below as many "action words" as you can find relating specifically to the things Ruth did. (There are several listed to get you started.)

go, glean, find,

BEHIND THE SCENES

Gleaning meant "to gather the grain after the harvesters." "The law required that farmers leave the corners of their plots to be harvested by the poor. See Leviticus 19:9; 23:22; Deut. 24:19."[7]

The season was late summer, the temperature hot, the air was dry and dusty, and the constant bending, lifting, and hauling was back-breakingly difficult. Yet describe Ruth's work habits as seen in verses 3, 7, 17 and 23.

Review Ruth 2. Think about the various meetings, conversations, and tasks, and describe your perception of Ruth's attitude during this season of her life.

Notice how Ruth was not necessarily an extraordinary gleaner or a shrewd businesswoman. She did not go to the fields and demand the rights that were hers as a widow. She simply began to work as best she knew how out of a willing heart and trusted God with the results of her labor. In the following verses found in Ruth 2, list how the Lord took her offering of service, gave her favor, and multiplied her efforts.

v. 8

v. 9

v. 12

v. 14

v. 15

v. 16

Read Ruth 2:1–3. We will later discover the significance of Ruth's meeting with Boaz, but for now, suffice it to say that it became a life-saving, future-changing event! Ruth's willingness to humble herself and remain faithful to the menial (but necessary) tasks at hand put her in a position to meet her destiny! How does God feel about our faithfulness? Read each Scripture verse below and write down the fruits of faithfulness.

Ps. 31:23

Ps. 101:6

Matt. 24:45–47

Matt. 25:21

Examine Ruth 2:3 again. In the New King James Version, a portion of that verse reads, ". . . and she <u>happened</u> to come to the part of the field *belonging* to Boaz. . . ." In other words, she was led directly to the place where her redemption could be fulfilled. What does this speak to you about finding God's will, choosing God's way over your own, and your faithfulness to fulfill the daily duties of life?

Remaining faithful to the work God puts before us can be a challenge to our flesh. We may become tired or discouraged. But the Lord understands that. Turn to 2 Thessalonians 3:6–13. Also read Galatians 6:6–9. Write out Galatians 6:9 below.

All that we do is "doing good" when it is done for the glory of God (1 Cor. 10:31). As we depend upon Him, have faith in His Word, pray for direction and blessing, and are motivated by our love for Christ, even common actions become fruitful and simple deeds holy! For "your labor is not in vain in the Lord" (1 Cor. 15:58).

 FAITH ALIVE

Take a few minutes and consider some of the less-than-glamorous responsibilities that are yours to fulfill. Are they dishes, laundry, ironing, and cleaning? Could it be an unfulfilling, but necessary, place of employment? What about the constant effort required for properly training your children? Your personal devotion to God? Opening your home in hospitality? All these require discipline and faithfulness, yet don't always show immediate fruit. As you prayerfully examine your own life, list some areas where you'd like to grow in faithfulness or feel "wearied in well doing." Then reevaluate your heart attitude toward the day-to-day responsibilities that are yours to fulfill. Write down the thoughts and feelings that the Holy Spirit brings to light.

Just examining your life and realizing truth is not always enough. Our life with God is a partnership. He is a gentleman and shows no partiality (Acts 10:34), so He will never force change upon us without an act of our will being involved. Thus it is essential that we *ask* of God those things that we desire of Him. Review your writings above, then lift those things to God in prayer. Be specific in what you desire from the Lord. If you want forgiveness for imperfect attitudes, confess that now to Jesus. If you need His refreshing touch to bring new life to the mundane, ask Him. If you desire Him to multiply your efforts, tell Him. We *can* be faithful, because *He* is faithful to enable us! Hallelujah!

Look now at Ruth 2:4–13. We will do a more in-depth study of these verses in the next chapter, but for the present, read verse 12 several times over. We asked in the introductory lesson, "From where did Ruth draw the strength and courage to remain faithful in the midst of difficulty?" What does this verse tell you that was obvious even to those who had only just encountered Ruth?

Herein lies the source of Ruth's strength, hope, and trust in God that allowed her to receive His redemption. She understood that though the realities of life can sometimes be harsh, unfair, or difficult to understand, there is that place of security, comfort, peace, and love: in the shadow of the wing of the Almighty God, abiding in His presence.

Open your Bible to Psalm 17:8. What do you think "keep me as the apple of Your eye" might mean?

    WORD WEALTH

Apple, *bath.* A daughter, apple, branch; from the word *banah,* to build, obtain children, repair.

The Hebrew word for *apple* in Psalm 17:8 is the same word used for *daughter* in Ruth (eight times). It is as though God is tenderly and specifically looking for His *daughters* to come and take refuge under the shadow of His wing.

FAITH ALIVE

Now turn in your Bible to Psalm 91 and read verses 1–16. Take a few moments and meditate on what it means to take refuge in God. Think of ways you can fit times of refuge with the Lord into your current life-style (in the early morning, during lunch break at work, before bed, and so on). Write down some realistic goals for taking time to abide faithfully as His daughter in His strengthening presence.

As you conclude this lesson, read Ruth 2:22, 23. Though it appears the immediate needs of Ruth and Naomi were met, they are by no means fully provided for. What were their immediate and long-term *needs*? List what you think some of their *desires* were, also.

Now read verse 23 again. How does it appear Ruth planned to fulfill those needs and desires?

1. *Spirit-Filled Life Bible* (Nashville, TN: Thomas Nelson Publishers, 1991), 386, "The Book of Ruth: Purpose."

2. Ibid., 389, note on 1:13.

3. Ibid., 389, note on 1:16, 17.

4. Ibid., 389, note on 1:18.

5. Ibid., 1532, note on 9:61, 62.

6. Ibid., 389, note on 1:21, 22.

7. Ibid., 390, note on 2:2.

Lesson 8/Ruth—Daughter of Redemption

We learned in the previous chapter how God views our faithfulness to the responsibilities of life, however large or seemingly insignificant they may seem. We saw that He honors and blesses the faithful, and intercepts us with His plan in the midst of our being diligent. Also realized was the importance of abiding in the Lord's presence, in order to find the strength to remain faithful. Let us now examine how Ruth's trusting response to God and faithfulness in her circumstances allowed redemption to be released in and through her life.

Read Ruth 2 again in its entirety.

In verses 1–3, we see Ruth continuing faithfully in the fields of Boaz. In verse 4, Boaz visits his field and will shortly encounter Ruth. Who, exactly, was this man Boaz? What was his significance to Ruth and Naomi?

To find out, first look at Ruth 4:21 and Matthew 1:5. Who were Boaz's mother and father?

Boaz would have been born sometime after the fall of Jericho. Considering the times of war and peace recorded in Judges and the ten years Naomi spent in Moab, Boaz would have been at least 40 years old.

Read Ruth 2:1. How was Boaz related to Naomi?

Notice also that this verse refers to Boaz as "a man of great wealth." In Hebrew, this "encompasses more than economic prosperity. It reflects the possessor's power and social standing in the community. It also indicates that Boaz was probably a warrior earlier in life."[1]

Remembering his mother's experience in Jericho (Josh. 2:1–21; 6:17–25) and the many other miracles both his mother and father would have experienced with the Israelites, what effect might that have had on Boaz's upbringing and values?

Now read Ruth 2:4–17 and 3:2, 10–15. Use these verses and what has already been studied and write as detailed a description as you can of Boaz.

In chapter 2, Boaz encounters Ruth for the first time, and her reputation has preceded her (2:11). Notice in verse 8, "'You will listen': Boaz appeals to Ruth's understanding as well as to her physical hearing of the words. He clearly wants her to sense his sincere concern for her well being."[2]

She is not only a woman at a time in history when a man would have very little to do with a woman in public, but she is also a foreigner, who would normally be looked down upon in Judah. To what can we attribute Boaz's amazing response? As Ruth put it in verse 10, "Why have I found favor in your eyes . . . ?"

Let us first look at the type of woman Ruth was.

 BEHIND THE SCENES

Her name, Ruth, has no exact Hebrew translation because of its Moabite origin. However, it could be derived from the word for friend or friendship ("reu"), an attribute Ruth had displayed with Naomi and which was known to Boaz (2:11). It could also have come from a contraction of "reuth" (in English, "a sight"), implying she was beautiful as well.

In any case, there were many other character qualities Ruth displayed that could have played a part in endearing her so quickly to Boaz. Read 2:7, 9, 10, 12, 17, 18, and 23, and list some of the qualities these verses reveal.

Boaz was kind and comforting to Ruth and went out of his way to see that her needs were met. What, then, was Ruth's response to such overt displays of generosity? Did she stiffen her neck with pride and refuse his help? Was she suspicious of his motives? Did resentment build because of her position of need? Did Ruth feel unqualified for Boaz's help? A "yes" to any of these attitudes would not have been unusual. Yet we've already examined Ruth's character and attitude and found it to be exemplary. Read Ruth 2:10, 13, 14, 21, and 23 again, and summarize Ruth's specific responses to Boaz.

What might the results have been for her and Naomi, if Ruth had been unwilling to listen to Boaz's direction and had not been open to receive his help?

What does Ruth 2:23 tell us she did instead?

In chapter 3, Naomi, out of her love for Ruth, again showed concern for the future and well-being of her daughter-in-law. Read Ruth 2:20 and 3:1, 2. What term did Naomi use in referring to Boaz?

BEHIND THE SCENES

The word "relative" refers to Boaz's position as one of Naomi's few remaining kinsmen from her husband's family. The Levirate law regarding the preservation of families (Lev. 25:25, 47–55) stated that a brother-in-law (*levir*) could be called upon by a widow to act as her husband and raise up a son to carry on the name of the deceased. In Ruth's case, because there were no brothers-in-law, the nearest relative could take on that role. He was also required to "redeem" her, or to buy back the land a woman was forced to sell when she became a widow. Hence, the term "kinsman-redeemer" encompasses the widow's full redemption to her original status.

Look up the word "restore" in the dictionary and write out its definition.

Naomi began to realize that Boaz could be God's redemption for Ruth, so she put together a bold but tender plan (see Ruth 3:1–4). "Naomi's direction and Ruth's ensuing action may appear to be seductive and inconsistent with the spiritual nobility of the book. To the contrary, however, Boaz's words, 'You *are* a virtuous woman' (3:11), make clear that he believed her to be highly moral."[3]

BEHIND THE SCENES

It is not clear why Naomi chose this exact method or time. It was nearing the end of harvest; Naomi may have realized Boaz would likely return to Bethlehem when the winnowing was completed. In fact, the "eating and drinking" referred to in Ruth 3:3 were likely the celebration feast, indicating the end of the harvest. Perhaps Naomi thought Ruth needed to approach Boaz before he left.

Ruth, as a Moabitess, was probably not fully versed in Israelite law regarding a kinsman, so she was wisely open to the counsel of the authority God had placed in her life. Ruth 3:5 records her specific response to Naomi's request. Write the verse below.

FAITH ALIVE

In the lesson of Sarah we saw submission as an act of faith. What can you add from Ruth's life regarding the proper spirit and attitude toward the people God places in authority over you?

Ruth 3:6–8 tells of what initially took place as Ruth visited Boaz. "'Uncovered his feet': The obvious purpose was that the chill of the night would naturally awaken him in time and occasion his discovering her at his feet. 'Was startled' may be translated 'shivered with cold.'"[4]

BEHIND THE SCENES

In verse 9, "'under your wing' is literally 'spread the corner of your garment over.' This is the most tender point of the account, and the most liable to misconstruction. The culture of the ancient Middle Eastern world involved the practice of the casting of a garment over one being claimed for marriage (see Ezek. 16:8), a tradition to which Ruth clearly refers. It does not imply anything so inappropriate as a midnight tryst."[5] Ruth was simply asking, "Since you are my nearest relative, I ask that you take me as your wife."

Verse 10 begins Boaz's response to Ruth's request. It was fairly obvious Boaz cared for Ruth. Why do you think he waited for Ruth to take the initiative and approach him first?

Ruth represents so much of what God desires for us as women, and here in verse 11 is yet another quality to which we can aspire. Who was aware of Ruth's reputation as a virtuous woman?

WORD WEALTH

Virtuous, *chayil.* A force; capable, strong; with valour, excellence, substance, might. "Virtuous" implies more than doing well; there is a strength and courage in spite of difficulties. It comes from the root word *chiyl,* which includes in its definition trust and waiting patiently. "Virtuous," then, is very close to "meekness"—a power and strength tempered by trusting patience.

Read the following scriptures and write after each one the results of a life lived virtuously before others.

Prov. 31:30, 31

Matt. 5:14–16

1 Pet. 2:11, 12

The Bible warns against the dangerous and frustrating trap of living to please and impress others (Prov. 29:25; John 12:42, 43). What Ruth exhibits here is a very different attitude. Her life is lived in a manner intent only on pleasing God, and that is what is impressive to others.

Things seemed to be going according to Naomi's plan. But suddenly, in 3:12, a wrinkle develops. What did Boaz know that apparently Ruth and Naomi did not?

What did Boaz promise Ruth in verse 13?

Now read verses 14–18. Boaz again displayed his concern for Ruth's welfare when he took every precaution to ensure her reputation. He first warned others not to talk about her visit. In verse 15, "the large measure [the six ephahs of barley] was not only an expression of Boaz's will to provide abundantly for her future (v. 17) but it also provided an apparent reason for Ruth's presence. People would conclude she came to secure a supply of grain to carry home prior to the heat of the day."[6]

Naomi had done all she knew to do before God, and Ruth had laid out her petition. What was left for them to do? (v. 18)

Read 2 Chronicles 20:17 and Psalm 46:10. Though there are times to take action and partner with God to see His purpose enacted, why do you think He sometimes has us be still and wait?

In Ruth 4, Boaz quickly took action on Ruth's behalf. He explained the situation to the nearer relative, who at first agreed to act as redeemer for Naomi. What happened when he discovered it also involved acting as Ruth's kinsman? (v. 6)

The man explained it could jeopardize his own inheritance by altering previous commitments within his own family. Why else might he have declined to fulfill his role (consider the cost, current family, Ruth's heritage, and so on)?

Boaz then seized the opportunity to step in as kinsman-redeemer. Ruth became his wife and was not only redeemed, loved, and provided for, but was given a son, Obed, a forefather in the lineage of the Messiah. Ruth was privileged with the exceptional honor of becoming a mother in the line of our ultimate Redeemer, Jesus Christ!

 BEHIND THE SCENES

"When something is restored in the Scriptures . . . it is always increased, multiplied or improved so that its latter state is significantly better than its original state (see Joel 2:21–26)."[7]

Record the people mentioned in Ruth 4:12.

An investigation of Tamar's experience sheds important light on the grace of God at work in women who have suffered or become exploited. Turn to Genesis 38 and read of the account of Tamar (vv. 6–30).

Who was Tamar's first husband, and what happened to him? (vv. 6, 7)

"Israel attributed both good and evil, life and death, to God (see Is.45:7). This premature death was a judgment for Er's undefined wickedness."[8]

Who was her second husband (v. 8) and what did he refuse to do? (v. 9)

What was his fate? (v. 10)

Tamar certainly experienced her share of pain and heartache after marrying into the family of Judah.

    BEHIND THE SCENES

According to Levirate law, Shelah, the next son of Judah, was to provide an heir through Tamar for his brother. Judah promised Tamar his third son, but he never followed through (38:26). Perhaps Tamar felt her only recourse was to produce an heir by Judah.

According to 38:13–25, summarize Tamar's trickery against Judah.

BEHIND THE SCENES

"The signet was a personal identification seal hanging from a cord about its owner's neck. The staff probably had a distinctive carving at the top. Tamar had a sense for the dramatic: she knew that anyone in the household could quickly identify their owner."[9]

What was the result of Tamar's plan? (38:27–30)

As shocking as Tamar's actions were in securing an heir, a fruitful race followed and became part of the Messiah's bloodline.

In light of the redemptive nature of God evidenced throughout the Book of Ruth, why do you think Tamar was included in this account? (Ruth 4:12)

Read Isaiah 58:1–14. What does this passage emphasize about repentance and restoration?

Now read Psalm 23:1–3.

WORD WEALTH

Soul, *nephesh.* A life, a living being; soul, self, person, mind, personality; inner desires and feelings. . . . "Soul" is the word usually chosen in translations for *nephesh,* but "heart," "person," "life," and "mind" are occasionally best suited to a particular context. Unlike the English word "soul," which usually describes only the inner person and is contrasted with the outer person, *nephesh* describes the whole person as a unit, that is a life, a living creation.[10]

In Psalm 23:3, what did David mean by "he restores my soul"?

BEHIND THE SCENES

The Old Testament contains many instances that are seen as a type, or a foreshadowing, of Jesus and His plan of redemption for mankind. But none are quite as tender and specific as found in Ruth, where Boaz so beautifully typifies the redeeming role of our Kinsman-Redeemer, the Lord Jesus Christ. A striking fact within the text is that there actually was another who normally would have taken on the role (3:12; 4:1–12); but because of fear, weakness, failure, or ignorance, he declined his position.

The Book of Ruth is a beautiful story of faithfulness and redemption, and models to women what to strive for in order to receive the Lord's restoration in their own lives:

1. To humbly continue in obedient and faithful service to all He calls you to.
2. To receive strength, security, and hope by daily abiding in the covering presence of the Almighty God.
3. To receive with gratitude the full redemption of all that's been lost from the hand of our Kinsman-Redeemer, the Lord Jesus Christ, whose greatest desire is to see you restored to wholeness, regardless of your background or past.

Feel free to add any further conclusions you may have received from your study in the Book of Ruth.

1. *Spirit-Filled Life Bible* (Nashville, TN: Thomas Nelson Publishers, 1991), 390, note on 2:1.
2. Ibid., 390, note on 2:8.
3. Ibid., 391, note on 3:3–5.
4. Ibid., note on 3:7, 8.
5. Ibid., 391–392, note on 3:9.
6. Ibid., 392, note on 3:15.
7. Ibid., 2012, "The Biblical Definition of Restoration."
8. Ibid., 61, note on 38:7.
9. Ibid., 62, note on 38:25.
10. Ibid., 896, "Word Wealth: 10:3 soul."

Lesson 9/ Esther—Daughter of Purpose

Romans 8:28 reads, "And we know that all things work together for good to those who love God, to those who are the called according to *His* purpose." In the Greek, the word *purpose* "suggests a deliberate plan, a proposition, an advance plan, an intention, a design."[1]

God is at work to cause events and circumstances to ultimately conclude for the good of His people. And often He uses us, His people, as agents in that process. We are at those times, then, part of His advance plan, fulfilling His purpose through our lives.

Esther apparently understood that, for she allowed herself to be used mightily of God for the purpose of saving her people, the Jews, from destruction. Let's look into the Word and find what it was about her that enabled God to use her for advancing His purpose. Studying Esther, what can we learn about fulfilling the purpose of God for our lives? Let's begin the discovery process now.

First, read the entire Book of Esther for an overview of her life. It doesn't take long and it's loaded with action! Record any questions you have below.

 BEHIND THE SCENES

Note the name of God does not appear even once in the book, as is also true in the Song of Solomon; but also note where His whispered presence and wise ways are constantly at work behind the scenes.

It will be helpful to understand the culture and structure of the government during the time of Esther in order to realize the decisions and situations are not as harsh or unfair as they may seem.

BEHIND THE SCENES

"The book takes its name from the beautiful, orphaned Jewess who became the queen of the Persian king Ahasuerus. He is generally believed to have been King Xerxes I who succeeded Darius I in 485 B.C. and ruled for twenty years over 127 provinces from India to Ethiopia. He lived in the Persian capital of Shushan. At this time a number of Jews were still in Babylon under Persian rule, even though they had been free to return to Jerusalem (Ezra 1; 2) for over fifty years. The story takes place over a period of four years, starting in the third year of Xerxes' reign."[2]

King Ahasuerus was the son of Darius, one of the mightiest rulers of all time. His empire had become the largest and wealthiest known to man. Raised in this atmosphere, Ahasuerus was a man accustomed to tremendous wealth and power and would not be questioned or crossed.

KINGDOM EXTRA

An encyclopedia (Bible or otherwise) would provide a place to begin a fascinating study of Darius, Ahasuerus (King Xerxes I) or the Persian Empire.

Now read Esther 1 and record the main events.

BEHIND THE SCENES

The six-month feast mentioned was likely a display of the king's wealth and power to bolster the morale of his people.

Under Darius they had suffered a crushing defeat in Greece at Marathon, despite their numerical superiority. They were soon to return again and make a second attempt at victory.

Why had the king requested Vashti's presence? (vv. 10, 11)

What caused the king's fury? (Esth. 1:12)

Notice in verse 9 that, at the time Vashti was called by the king, she was feasting with the women. Do you think this could have influenced her decision to deny the king? Why or why not?

Why might the king have desired support at this time, especially from Vashti?

What was the main worry of the king and his advisors? (vv. 15–18)

Read 1 Corinthians 5:6 and Hebrews 12:15. Do you think King Ahasuerus and his advisors had reason for concern?

Vashti was in a unique position. She was not just refusing her husband; she had chosen to deny the king. Some might applaud her as a courageous woman with her own mind. Others might feel it was within her right to refuse her husband's request. Still others might be appalled at her contempt for the king's request.

FAITH ALIVE

Our responses to authority are shaped by various circumstances and experiences and reflect many things about us. Choose five words that best describe your response to authority now in your life (for example, "anger," "responsiveness," "fear," "trust," "resentment").

What can you conclude about yourself from this?

You may want to add these conclusions to your personal prayer list, your praise report list, or both!

Read Esther 2 and list the main characters.

 BEHIND THE SCENES

Several years passed. King Ahasuerus had led an even larger campaign, over 100,000 men, against Greece, only to be humiliated again by defeat. He must have felt keenly the need for support and encouragement.

How does it appear the king felt about Vashti then? (2:1)

Because any decree of the king was irrevocable (8:8), there was nothing he could do regarding his loss of Vashti. What was the plan of the king's servants in 2:2–4?

It is here we first encounter Mordecai and Esther. According to verses 5 and 6, who was Mordecai?

 FAITH ALIVE

In 586 B.C., Kish (v. 5) was taken from Judah to Babylon. When Cyrus, a Persian king, conquered Babylon, he moved many Jews to Susa (Shushan). Some still resided there, including Mordecai, although they had been freed to return to Jerusalem more than fifty years before (see Ezra 1; 2).

PROBING THE DEPTHS

For a more detailed examination on how the Jews ended up in Susa (Shushan), read 2 Kings 24; 25; 2 Chronicles 36; and Ezra 1; 2.

How was Mordecai related to Esther? (2:7)

Read Esther 2:7, 10, 11, 20; 4:4, 5–17; 8:1, 2 and describe what you perceive of Mordecai and Esther's relationship.

How is Esther described in Esther 2:7?

WORD WEALTH

Beautiful, *towb.* Good, beautiful, best, bountiful, cheerful, glad, gracious, kind, loving, pleasant, precious, ready, sweet. A much broader, encompassing definition of beauty, implying far more than the outward physical features.

Compare the beauty ascribed to Esther with Vashti's. Read Esther 2:9, 10, 15, 17, 20; 4:4, 5, 16; 7:2–4; 8:3. Combining all this information, form a list of words to describe Esther and her character.

What took place in 2:8–16 was akin to an ancient beauty pageant! The kingdom was searched for the most beautiful of virgins, and they were prepared and brought before the king.

Esther 2:15 shows the astute wisdom balanced with gracious humility that Esther possessed. What happened with Hegai?

What does the Bible record about receiving counsel? Look up these passages and write a brief summary next to each reference.

Ex. 18:19–24

1 Kin. 12:8–16

Prov. 1:5; 11:14; 19:20

FAITH ALIVE

A practical way to live by the counsel of the wise is to be prepared in advance. Sit down with your spouse, parents, or those you are most closely associated with and comprise a list of those believers in Christ from whom you would most readily receive counsel (your "counsel council"!). The list can include your pastor, elders, friends, family, financial advisors, and so on. Make them aware that you look to them for leadership. Pray for them regularly. Then when a challenge or crisis presents itself, you are not scrambling to figure out what to do, but ready with "a multitude of counselors [for] safety" (Prov. 11:14).

Esther 2:17, 18 shows there was a quality in Esther's life that was evident even to the king. Raised in the home of the devout Israelite, Mordecai, the difference of her godly and gracious manner was likely magnified in the presence of the idolatrous Persian women. What was the result? (vv. 17, 18)

Read Esther 2:19–23. As many as five years had passed, and as if the account of Esther were not compelling enough, we come to this dramatic subplot. Hold it in your mind, as it will be significant later.

Now read Esther 3.

 BEHIND THE SCENES

Haman was an Amalekite and a descendant of Agag, the ruler who was spared by Saul in disobedience to God (1 Sam. 15). The Amalekites had long been enemies of Israel, even attacking them during their journey to the Promised Land (Ex. 17:8–14; Deut. 25:17–19).

Summarize Haman's plot against the Jews. (Notice it included those not only in Shushan, but in all 127 provinces. It was to be an Old Testament holocaust.)

How did Haman deceive the king? (Esth. 3:8, 9)

Why do you think Mordecai refused to bow to Haman? (vv. 2–4)

This apparently disturbed Haman to the point that he wanted all Jews in Persia destroyed. Why was he not content with just Mordecai's death?

Now read Esther 4:1–12. The Jews had received word of the plan (to be carried out 11 months later)[3] against them and were mourning their fate. What was Esther's response to their pain? (v. 4)

Now read Romans 12:15 and Colossians 3:12, 13. Why is compassion an important quality to possess?

What was Esther's initial reaction (4:11) to Mordecai's request of verse 8?

It was at this point (4:12–17) that Esther could have taken the easy way, the "wide road" (Matt. 7:13, 14). She could have finessed and charmed her way into a place of personal safety through the king's favor (5:3, 6); and, indeed, would have thwarted the purpose of God for her own life through selfish ambition or outright disobedience to what she knew was right to do. But she heeded the profound voice of Mordecai. Write the last sentence of 4:14 below.

"Esther's response is the ultimate commitment to Mordecai and her people, the condemned Jews. In essence, she says, 'You do your part to help me; and I will do what you have said, even if I die doing it.'"[4]

What all did Esther stand to lose by laying aside her own dreams and desires to aid God's people? (Think hard, and be as thorough as you can.)

She knew of only one source from which to draw the courage and strength to face the king. Where did she turn? (4:16)

Though Esther's works are evident in her fasting and prayer, 4:16 demonstrates her firm faith in the mercy and providence of God. What does that say to you about the balance of faith in God and our works on His behalf? (James 2:17, 18)

Read Esther 5 and summarize the events.

In verse 2, "the scepter was the rod (often ornate) of a ruler, symbolizing his power. When the king extends the scepter, he offers entrance and favor. When Esther touches the top of the scepter, she gratefully acknowledges her acceptance of the king's proffered grace. We can petition our God and King in prayer on the basis of His invitation to us (see Heb. 4:16)."[5]

Though she had prepared herself in every way possible, what does the king perceive in Esther before she even speaks? (v. 3)

In verse 8, the fruit of Esther's fasting and prayer becomes evident, as she "is being used wisely and shrewdly by God (see Matt. 10:16). She understands the importance of waiting for God's timing before making her request (see Eccl. 8:5, 6)."[6]

Now read Esther 5:9–14. Haman continued to exalt himself and resented Mordecai's lack of adoration. How did his wife, Zaresh, encourage her husband's vanity and wickedness?

Read Esther 6 and record the highlights.

Why do you think King Ahasuerus couldn't sleep? (6:1)

Notice in verse 1 how "God sovereignly intervenes, showing that He has numerous ways to see that His will is carried out for His obedient children (see Job 42:2; Ps. 57:2)."[7]

BEHIND THE SCENES

The "records of the chronicles" in 6:1 (and in 2:23) refers to a log book kept for the king to record the many significant events, decisions, appointments, and so on, that he decreed or that affected the kingdom. It is not to be confused with the 1 and 2 Chronicles of the Scripture. Considering the vast nature of the king's chronicles, the chances of the reader turning right to the events of Mordecai are slight. Truly God is quietly at work!

Read Galatians 6:6–9. Apply this passage first to Haman and then to Mordecai, and write down the different application to each of them.

Do you think Mordecai had "lost heart" (Gal. 6:9) when he went unnoticed in his deed of service to the king? (Esth. 2:19–23) Why or why not?

Do you think the timing of his reward was of the Lord? Explain.

Haman sought out recognition; what motivated Mordecai's actions?

Read Matthew 6:3, 4. Write your conclusions about service to God versus rewards.

What was Zaresh beginning to realize as she discovered Mordecai's heritage? (6:13)

Why do you think she would say this?

FAITH ALIVE

The power of God on behalf of His people was evident even to the wicked. The Jews often faced perilous times, as we do today. The temptation is to recoil in fear and to wish you had been born at another time or lived in another place. But God, in His wisdom, has given you to the kingdom for this very time. You need not fear, for He will keep you, sustain you and fulfill His purpose through you (Job 42:2; Ps. 57:1–3). You only need walk in obedience and faithful commitment before Him (2 Tim. 1:12).

God has placed me in this season,
Known to Him alone the reason.
Mine is but to seek His will
And be faithful to fulfill
His appointed plan for me
As He guides my destiny.[8]

Now read Esther 7, taking particular notice of how Esther spoke to King Ahasuerus (vv. 3, 4).

"The king's loss" in verse 4 could have referred to "Haman's inability to make up for the loss of revenue from the Jews' taxes."[9] What else might Esther have meant?

Why do you think the king left Esther and went into the palace garden? (v. 7) Why didn't Esther follow him?

FAITH ALIVE

In verse 8, "Haman's anxiety causes him to violate palace etiquette by being too close to the couch on which Esther reclined to eat. 'They covered Haman's face' as a sign of his being condemned to death."[10]

FAITH ALIVE

Esther showed extreme poise, self-control, and wisdom in a very tense and difficult situation. Take a moment and reflect on the atmosphere, her tone, and her attitude. Reread her words to the king (7:3, 4). Now think of yourself in a difficult or confrontational situation with someone in authority over you. What can you learn from Esther and apply to your own life? (James 1:22–25)

PROBING THE DEPTHS

For more on self-control, read Proverbs 14:29; 16:32; 17:14; Ecclesiastes 7:9; Galatians 5:22–26; James 1:19, 20.

Haman is then confronted and dealt with swiftly (Esth. 7:7–10). What was the tragic irony of Zaresh's wicked counsel? (5:14; 7:10)

Chapter 8 begins with the rewarding of both Esther and Mordecai for their selfless devotion to the king. But the problem of his irrevocable decree remains (v. 8). What plan did Esther and Mordecai develop to help the Jews? (vv. 3–11)

According to 8:9, Haman's law had stood seventy days. Given its original eleven-month term, the Jewish people had almost nine months to prepare their defense. What amazing reversals take place in that time? (v. 17)

Now read chapters 9 and 10. In this remaining portion of the book, we read of the fulfillment of Esther's divine purpose through the salvation and victory of her people. The Feast of Purim is also established, a two-day celebration during which the Book of Esther is to be read in its entirety. What reason is given for the remembrance? (9:26–28)

 FAITH ALIVE

It is important to record and review the testimonies of God's faithfulness and goodness. That is one reason we read and study God's Word. In addition, you might consider keeping a personal "Record of God's Goodness," in which you chronicle the times God has sovereignly met you or a family member. Keep track of such things as miraculous provision, a healing touch, an answered prayer, or divine protection. Then review that periodically with your family, perhaps at Thanksgiving or another special holiday (Ps. 34:1–4).

Esther did make several rather controversial requests that seemed almost vindictive (9:13). Why do you think she did this?

Even if her motive was impure, keep in mind the gospel of the Cross that requires forgiveness of enemies was not yet known. If nothing else, it is evidence that, even with all her admirable qualities, Esther was still but flesh. We can in that take hope, knowing that though she was ordinary and subject to the desires of the flesh, God still used her in an extraordinary fashion.

As this lesson concludes, take a few minutes and review your notes and think about Esther's life. Then answer the following questions.

Was it coincidence, accident, or providence that caused Esther to be raised to such a position? Explain your answer.

"Even in the presence of recognition, success, wealth, and luxury—an environment many may covet, but which has so often proven destructive to spiritual commitment"[11]—what was it that caused Esther to retain her perspective and integrity?

It was in losing her life that Esther actually found her purpose. Read Matthew 16:25. The temptation is to think, "If only my life could be spent in such grand significance, as was Esther's." But the truth is that, at every turn, there are opportunities to deny ourselves (lose our lives) for the sake of others. Only God Himself knows the eternal value of laying down your life to support your husband, raise a child, teach a Sunday school class, or witness to a neighbor. The point is to serve Him to your utmost where He has placed you, and that preparation will lead to a broader influence if such is His desire for you. God has given you to His kingdom for *today*. Let that be what guides your every deed, and you cannot help but fulfill His purpose for you.

1. *Spirit-Filled Life Bible* (Nashville, TN: Thomas Nelson Publishers, 1991), 1701, "Word Wealth: 8:28 purpose."

2. Ibid., 695, "Esther: Background and Date."

3. Ibid., 700, note on 3:13.

4. Ibid., 701, note on 4:16.

5. Ibid., 701, note on 5:2.

6. Ibid., note on 5:8.

7. Ibid., 702, note on 6:1.

8. Copyright © M. Wendy Parrish, 1993. Used by permission.

9. *Spirit-Filled Life Bible,* 703, note on 7:4.

10. Ibid., note on 7:8.

11. Ibid., 700, "Kingdom Dynamics: Rising to Meet Your Destiny (Esther)."

Lesson 10 Mary— Daughter and Mother

Through the ages, there have been women who have represented the ideals to which we all should aspire. But none have had as profound or eternal an impact as a modest Jewish maid, who bore from her body the Redeemer of the world.

This mother among mothers, as well as many other women in the Bible, model to us the great privilege and high calling of the unique gift of God to women alone—motherhood.

Some of us, though, may not have had the privilege of being a mother. Yet even if you have no children of your own, there is much to be gleaned from a closer look at the mothers of the Bible. Among the many principles found, there are three that can readily be seen. First, to understand the comfort of a mother's love is to know more fully the tender heart of God (Is. 66:13). Second, to give that love away to another, particularly children you may know or be related to, is much needed and welcomed. And third, to share what you have learned with a young, desperate mother could be a help beyond measure.

Open your Bible to Luke 1 and read verses 26–56. Write down any questions, observations, or key verses you'd like to note.

Mary was truly a role model in her humility, obedience, fidelity, and devotion as a woman, wife, and mother. However, this study will focus on the nine key elements that we see in Mary's example of godly motherhood.

THE PRIORITY

What do Luke 1:28 and 30 tell us about Mary and the Lord?

What does verse 38 further reveal about their relationship?

How does Mary refer to God in Luke 1:47?

It is apparent Mary understood the priority of knowing God and His ways, and she put Him above all other desires in her life. It was from that same rich well of relationship that she drew the wisdom and grace to nurture Jesus and her other children in the ways of the Lord.

What was the relationship of Mary and Joseph at the time of the angel's visitation? (Luke 1:27)

"Betrothal [engagement] was as binding as the actual marriage and could only be broken by divorce."[1] Mary had already betrothed herself to Joseph. How did her divine appointment change her commitment to him?

Did it change Joseph's commitment to Mary? (Matt. 1:18–25) Explain.

The Bible record gives no indication of Mary's commitment to the Lord or her husband changing when Jesus and her other children were born. What can you conclude about the order of Mary's priorities as a mother?

The most lasting gift a mother can give her children is to live according to God's order: to first love the Lord with all her heart (Deut. 10:12), love and honor her husband in the same fashion (Col. 3:12–14; Eph. 5:33), *then* love and cherish her children (Titus 2:4). When those priorities are confused, there can be sorrowful consequences.

 KINGDOM EXTRA

For an example of the effects of a mother putting her children first, review the story of Isaac and Rebekah in Genesis 24:1—28:5.

THE PRIVILEGE

Read Luke 1:28. The angel of the Lord addresses Mary as the "highly favored *one* . . . blessed . . . among women." What do you think this meant?

Mothers can also consider themselves as "highly favored," for they are uniquely privileged with the high calling of bringing forth life. But why do mothers have children? And do children belong to us just because we have them?

First turn to Genesis 1:26–28. Summarize God's original intention for humankind.

In addition, "God created man to be His kingdom agent, to rule and subdue the rest of creation, including aggressive satanic forces, which would soon infringe upon it."[2] So women have the privilege of bearing these future agents for God's kingdom.

Now turn to Luke 2:41–50. Where did Jesus go with His parents? (v. 41)

What happened to Jesus? (vv. 43–45)

"Villagers who made pilgrimages to Jerusalem usually traveled in caravans, with women and children in front. Each parent thought that Jesus was with the other."[3]

After three days, where did they finally find Jesus? (v. 46)

Jesus had apparently not tried to find them, and His parents voiced their anxiety (v. 48). What was His response? (v. 49)

Though Joseph and Mary did not understand what He meant, "Jesus shows an awareness of His unique relationship to the Father, as well as a consciousness of His mission."[4]

Jesus left the temple with His parents and remained in subjection to them (Luke 2:51). And though it was apparent He needed their nurture and care in His formative years (v. 52), to whom did He ultimately belong? (2:40)

According to 1 Corinthians 6:19, 20 and Colossians 1:16, to whom do *we* belong? Explain.

Psalm 127:3 tells us that "children *are* a heritage," meaning *they belong to God*. He has a destiny and purpose for *each* of them (Rom. 8:28). Therefore, the privilege of motherhood rests not just in the *bearing* of children. The true privilege comes from being entrusted with the faithful stewardship of the life-gifts of God, who will one day act as His agents, both now and through eternity (Rev. 5:10; 22:5).

THE PRAYER

Look at Luke 1:29, 30. Mary was troubled by what the angel was saying. What words did he use to comfort her? (v. 30)

What does Psalm 55:22 remind us to do with our burdens (fears)?

What, in turn, does the Lord promise?

 WORD WEALTH

Sustain, *chul.* To maintain, nourish, provide food, bear, hold up, protect, support, defend; to supply the means necessary for living.[5]

Jesus is able to touch our situations no matter how overwhelming they may seem and to sustain us by the same power with which He upholds the universe (Heb. 1:3). We only need call upon Him. But prayer for our children is certainly not limited to times of crisis alone. (Read Gen. 25:21–24 and 1 Sam. 1:1–28 for further insights.)

Jesus also demonstrated the importance of praying for children. Summarize the account in Matthew 19:13–15.

God gives a mother unique insight and discernment regarding the needs of her children; and it is her privilege and duty to bring those things before the Lord in prayer.

 FAITH ALIVE

Can you think of specific things currently on your heart that you'd like to see the Lord do in or for your children? Take some time this week to bring your requests to the Heavenly Father. Write them in a prayer notebook and continue to lift them up before the Lord until you've received His answer. Like Hannah, thank the Lord for the gift of your children and for His faithfulness to you and them. Begin to make prayer for your children a regular part of your devotional life.

THE PURPOSE

Now read Luke 1:31–33. The angel was very clear regarding the purpose intended for Jesus. And God also has a clear purpose for your children—and for you as their mother.

Turn to Luke 2:1–7. Joseph and Mary had traveled almost seventy miles in a most primitive fashion to a crowded city where the only resting place was a barn. It is here the Savior entered the world He was soon to redeem. What did Mary do with Jesus when He was born? (v. 7)

This so tenderly depicts the primary purpose of parents. It is not to provide every luxury and comfort, but to "wrap" (cover, love, hold, protect) their children.

Turn to Hosea 11:1–4. In this passage, "God reveals Himself as a Father who is tender, close to His children, and sensitive to their needs—teaching, encouraging, helping, and healing them. Growing up is not something that He leaves to chance. He is a God who conscientiously *nurtures* His children. . . . [Likewise], God entrusts children to parents, allowing His own nurturing heart to flow through them to the children."[6]

Do you think the newborn Jesus was aware of their difficult circumstances in Bethlehem?

Do you think He knew as a babe the terror of why they later fled to Egypt? (Matt. 2:3–16)

It is doubtful He did, for He had the loving protection of His parents surrounding Him. Even the God of the universe incarnate needed a loving, stable home for protection and security. But the purpose of God for mothers goes even beyond their tender love and care.

What is the scriptural directive of Proverbs 22:6?

"'Train up' has the idea of a parent graciously investing in a child whatever wisdom, love, nurture, and discipline is needed for him to become fully committed to God. It presupposes the emotional and spiritual maturity of the parent to do so. 'In the way he should go' is to train according to the unique personality, gifts, and aspirations of the child. It also means to train the child to avoid whatever natural tendencies he might have that would prevent total commitment to God (for example, a weak will, a lack of discipline, [moodiness])."[7]

Throughout the Bible, the training of children often rested with the mother, as is still true today. This by no means precludes the importance of the father's involvement (Eph. 6:4). But the reality is that the primary care-giver will have the most opportunity for influence, and that is usually the mother. Though this role is one that requires diligent commitment, the fruit of a mother's labor can have a profound impact.

Turn to 2 Kings 5:1–14. Namaan, a commander in Syria, had leprosy. His wife's maid was an Israelite girl who had been seized in a raid. What was the young maiden's advice to him? (v. 3)

What does that speak of the spiritual nurturing she received from her family in Israel before her capture?

What was the result of her readiness of faith? (vv. 14, 15)

Now turn to Proverbs 31:1. From where did Lemuel learn his wise observations?

Turn now to 2 Timothy 1:1–5. Whom does Paul credit with the evangelist Timothy's faith?

Why was Timothy so strong in faith and wise in the Scriptures? (2 Tim. 3:14, 15)

God has purposed many things for His daughters, but none as full of potential as the faithful nurturing and training of the next generation.

THE POWER

Turn to Luke 1 and read verses 34 and 35. Mary said to the angel, "How can this be . . . ?" Many mothers may ask themselves a similar question. "How can this be done? How can I shape a vessel that will be fit for the Master's use?"

By whose power was the miracle of Mary's conception performed? (v. 35)

Is that same power available to us today? (Zech. 4:10; Acts 1:8) Explain.

"The Holy Spirit is the Person and the Power by which assistance and ability are given for serving, for sharing the life and power of God's Kingdom with others. . . ,"[8] including our children. And with the power of the Spirit comes fruit. Look up Galatians 3:22, 23. Choose at least three things from this verse that you could use more of when it comes to properly training your children.

But being an effective mother requires even more. Turn back to Luke 1:34. In Mary's simple question, she showed she accepted the limitations of her human understanding, and asked for God's wisdom as to how this could be done. What does James 1:5 tell us to do if we need God's wisdom?

How is it given?

It is important to remember that human (fleshly) wisdom is woefully inadequate. This applies especially to the many theories and philosophies presented today about child-raising, which are subject to current trends and cultural biases. There is only one source of wise, unchanging truth—God's Word. And *all* advice on raising children should be in strict alignment with it.

For example, what does Ephesians 6:1 tell us is reasonable to expect from children?

What does Proverbs 13:24 tell us about loving children?

How could Ephesians 5:1–7 help to teach children about values?

God, through His Word, has given us a *complete* resource for shaping and training His children (2 Pet. 1:2–4). It is essential that a mother embrace its truth and apply it with wisdom by the power of the Holy Spirit.

 KINGDOM EXTRA

There are innumerable Bible-based resources that can help you use God's Word to wisely train your children, including books and audio/video tapes. Check with your pastor, or ask at your local Christian bookstore or a nearby Christian college library.

THE PARTICIPATION

Read Luke 1:36. In the tender timing of God, Elizabeth had a similar experience (Luke 1:5–25), and was able to help Mary work through what had happened. And Mary readily received the support of her cousin and friend (Luke 1:39–56).

Titus 2:3–5 exhorts older women to "admonish" (teach) the younger women. What are they to teach them? (vv. 4, 5)

By implication, the wisdom and skills necessary for godly mothering are something young women need assistance with. It can at times be a lonely and difficult struggle.

FAITH ALIVE

If you're a mother with young children, seek out an older relative or church member who can encourage you, pray for you, and teach you the ways of a godly mother. If you're a more experienced mom, look for young women who appear to be without that kind of help. It is something God directs in His Word, and it will be a mutual blessing.

THE POSSIBILITY

Write out Luke 1:37.

With the many questions and doubts likely swirling around Mary's mind, what a comforting reminder the angel brings! And what a comforting word for us as well! God is very aware of the challenges mothers with children face today. And they are not unique to the twentieth century.

Turn to 2 Kings 18:1, 2. In this passage, who was beginning his reign in Israel?

Who was this new ruler's mother? (v. 2)

BEHIND THE SCENES

His father, Ahaz, was a wicked king who had led the people into idolatry (which included the sacrificing of children), and who bribed foreign kings with items from the temple and dismantled other items to build a pagan altar. For more on the rule of King Ahaz, read 2 Kings 16.

In contrast to his father, how did Hezekiah rule? (2 Kin. 18:3–8)

In spite of his faithless father, Hezekiah "did *what was right* in the sight of the LORD" and was instrumental in bringing about a national spiritual revival. What can you conclude about the influence of his God-fearing mother, the daughter of Zechariah?

We have already learned of the influence of Eunice over her son Timothy; and this was in spite of the fact that her husband was a nonbeliever (Acts 16:1).

Though their lives are not without difficulty or trial, what can you conclude about families with only one believing parent?

Now turn to Genesis 21:14–21. Hagar, by her own insolence, had been sent away from the home of Abraham and faced the world as a mother alone with her son. What was God's response to their desperate situation?

What else does God's Word reveal about the plight of the fatherless? (Ex. 22:22, 23; Ps. 146:9)

Summarize what you've learned about God's heart toward single parents.

Other conditions also exist that strain the role of motherhood. Turn to Luke 2:22–24. Joseph and Mary were taking Jesus to the temple for His dedication. What did they bring as a sacrifice? (v. 24)

"This sacrifice is of the kind prescribed for the poor (Lev. 12:8),"[9] who do not possess the means to bring a lamb.

Joseph and Mary were poor. Because of their enforced exile in Egypt, good education was not available to their family. It's likely their only book was the Old Testament. Yet not only Jesus, but all of their children were taught of the Lord (Is. 54:13) and used by God (Acts 1:14). Children can grow up without many things or advantages—but proper training, nurturing, and love are not among them.

Now turn to Luke 2:34, 35. What did Simeon prophesy that Mary would experience?

The events leading up to Jesus' crucifixion must have torn at the very heart of Mary. He was falsely accused, beaten, humiliated, and despised. "The opposition to Jesus [reached] its climax at the Cross, where Mary [experienced] piercing anguish."[10]

But what was Mary's physical posture as she watched her Son's death? (Luke 23:49)

She had experienced His miracles and heard His proclamations. She must have known He was truly the Redeemer and *stood* in the knowledge that God was in control.

FAITH ALIVE

You may be a mother who has been pierced in her soul. Perhaps there has been a spiritual death blow dealt to a child of yours who is now no longer walking in the will and purpose of God. Know this day that the resurrection power of the Lord Jesus Christ is available to you. You wrestle against the powers of hell, but the victory has already been won. Put on the whole armor of God and, like Mary, *stand* in faith (Eph. 6:10–17). Continue to contend in faithful intercession, remembering that "with God nothing will be impossible" (Luke 1:37).

THE PRICE

Read Luke 1:38. Write down Mary's response to what God was requiring of her.

To be a faithful mother, one *must* be an obedient disciple. Only God knows His plans for your children; thus, it is essential that you follow His leading and directives for raising them. Because "children will do as you do, not as you say," what more loving example than to live before them a life of obedience to Christ (1 John 5:2)?

Mary called herself a "maidservant" of the Lord (Luke 1:38). Define what you think she meant by that.

Now read Matthew 20:25–28. The Son of Man did not come to be served; for what two reasons did He come?

Jesus came willingly, and though it cost Him everything, the purpose for God's children was fulfilled through His sacrifice. With Jesus as our example, define the sacrificial service of motherhood.

Because a mother may not see the immediate fruit of her service, she may become discouraged or discontent and seek other means for fulfillment. What does Hebrews 13:5, 6 tell us about contentment?

What can be added from 1 Timothy 6:6?

Motherhood is not something we are called to either *resent* or *defend*; but to joyfully *accept* (Luke 1:38) as the provision of God for our redemption (Gen. 3:15; 1 Tim. 2:13–15) and our children's blessing. The calling of God is irrevocable (Rom. 11:29) and does not change, regardless of the culture or modern trends (Num. 23:19; Heb. 13:8). The role of a mother is a high calling of honor and privilege and should never be regarded as anything less.

THE PRAISE

Finally, read Luke 1:45. Mary *believed* and trusted in the almighty power and faithfulness of God, enough so to spend her life in service and devotion to His kingdom (1:38).

What was Mary's final response to all that God was asking of her? (1:46–55)

Turn to Psalm 145:1–3. How often should we bless and praise the Lord? (v. 2)

To whom should we declare His mighty acts? (v. 4)

"This verse emphasizes the importance of passing on the praise of God from one generation to another. Praise is to be taught to our children. . . . We must not merely 'suppose' that children will grow up and desire God. We must be careful. Whatever we possess of God's blessing and revelation can be lost in one generation. We must consistently praise Him and we must also teach (by example, as well as by words), so our children and our children's children will do the same."[11]

A mother is blessed in the sight of God, especially when she understands the priority, privilege, prayer, purpose, power, participation, possibility, price, and praise involved in her faithful service to Him as a steward of His children.

Review this lesson, and write down any final observations, follow-up questions, or prayer requests.

1. *Spirit-Filled Life Bible* (Nashville, TN: Thomas Nelson Publishers, 1991), 1405, note on 1:18, 19.

2. Ibid., 5, note on 1:26.

3. Ibid., 1513, note on 2:44.

4. Ibid., note on 2:49.

5. Ibid., 801, "Word Wealth: 55:22 sustain."

6. Ibid., 1270, "Kingdom Dynamics: God's Nurturing Heart in Parents Flows to Children."

7. Ibid., 912, note on 22:6.

8. Ibid., 1622, "Kingdom Dynamics: Receiving Kingdom Power."

9. Ibid., 1511, note on 2:24.

10. Ibid., 1512, note on 2:35.

11. Ibid., 876, "Kingdom Dynamics: Teach Your Children Praise."

Lesson 11/Priscilla—Daughter of Virtue

"Who can find a virtuous wife?" asks the writer of Proverbs 31. This chapter sets forth "the high standard for womanhood, apparently drawn not by some romantic male, but by one who was herself a virtuous woman"[1] (Prov. 31:1). This lesson will examine more closely the qualities of the virtuous woman (for it includes principles applicable to more than just wives) and how they were reflected in the lives of Priscilla and other wives of the Bible.

But while studying, keep in mind that the commandments of the Lord "are not burdensome" (1 John 5:3). Before being tempted to feel condemned or weighed down by the seemingly unattainable standards of Proverbs 31, understand that they are intended as inspiring goals. And, though *attainable*, they do require time, effort, prayer, and the working of God through grace to become fully operational in one's life. Remember, "I **can** do all things through Christ who strengthens me" (Phil. 4:13).

Begin by reading Proverbs 31:10–31. Write down any questions or other notations as you read.

Because Priscilla will be held up as a model throughout the course of this lesson, you may want to familiarize yourself with the references to her in Scripture. Read Acts 18:2–4, 18, 19, 24–26; Romans 16:3–5; 1 Corinthians 16:19; and 2 Timothy 4:19. (Place markers in your Bible at these locations, as you will turn to them often.) Note your observations regarding Priscilla—first as a woman, and then as a wife.

Now read Proverbs 31:10. It is apparent that a wife of virtue (excellence) is an unusually rare thing, and certainly to be valued if found. Adam most assuredly valued the companionship of Eve, but what was God's purpose in creating a woman for him? (1 Cor. 11:9)

Turn to Genesis 2:18–24. According to verse 18, why did God make women?

"'A helper' indicates that Adam's strength for all he was called to be and do was inadequate in itself. [The New King James Version reads] 'comparable to him', [denoting] complementarity. The needed help is for daily work, procreation, and mutual support through companionship."[2]

When God made woman, what does Genesis 2:22 tell us He did with this gift for Adam?

According to verse 24, what were the conditions of their union?

 WORD WEALTH

Joined, *proskollao.* To glue or cement together, stick to, adhere to, join firmly. . . . [It] includes faithfulness, loyalty, and permanency in relationships.[3]

"'Leave' connotes a priority change on the part of the husband. 'Be joined' has the idea of both passion and permanence. 'One flesh' carries a number of implications, including sexual union, child conception, spiritual and emotional intimacy, and showing each other the same respect shown other close kin, such as one's parents or siblings."[4]

Write as complete a summary as you can on God's original purpose and role for a wife.

Now turn to 1 Corinthians 11:3. "The relationship between God as 'Head' and Christ as Son is given as a model for the relationship between husband and wife. When the Bible reveals how the Father and the Son relate to each other, it also tells us something about the way that husbands and wives should relate to each other."[5]

Match the following scripture references to the principles illustrated for marriage in the relationship of Jesus and the Father.

share a mutual love	John 5:22; 16:15
have different roles and functions	John 8:29
different roles, but equal	John 5:20; 14:31
live in unity	John 11:42
esteem one another	John 10:30
shared life and ministry	John 14:9, 11
attentive to one another	John 8:49, 54
care for one another	John 10:17; 14:28; 17:46

Proverbs 31:10 also says a good wife is valued "far above rubies," or is an invaluable resource to her husband. Accord-

ing to Acts 18:3, 18, 24–26 and Romans 16:3–5, how do you think Priscilla was of high value to Aquila?

Notice also how Aquila and Priscilla are *always* listed together, never one without the other. What does this speak to you about their relationship?

Take a moment and list things a godly wife can do or be that are of high value to her husband.

Now read Proverbs 31:11. How does a wife gain her husband's confidence and trust?

Turn first to Ephesians 5:22–33. Notice how "these verses put such demands upon the Christian husband that it is impossible to see how a charge of male chauvinism could justly be made against the Bible, or how a license to exploit wives could ever be claimed."[7] But the Bible also has its requirements of a wife. What three things is she asked to do? (vv. 22, 24, 33)

We saw in the life of Sarah how submission was established by God out of His all-wise and loving care, and aligns a woman under her husband while also placing her under the larger canopy of God's divine order and blessing.

What does the Bible give as a model for a wife in showing respect (reverence) to her husband? (Eph. 5:24)

Hence, she is to "acknowledge [the husband's] calling as 'head' of the family, respond to his leadership, listen to him, praise him, be unified in purpose and will with him; be a true helper. . . . No [wife] can do this by mere willpower or resolve, but since you are 'His workmanship' (Eph. 2:8–10), God will help bring this about."[8]

In light of what has just been studied, does respect have to be earned, or should it be given voluntarily? Why?

Now turn to Romans 15:7. This verse is directed to Christians in general, but can apply to marriage as well. Write it out.

"'Receive' means 'to take to oneself.' Its root indicates strong action toward us—that in Christ, God literally came to us and <u>took hold of us</u> 'while we were yet sinners' (Rom. 5:8). By that act of acceptance He released the grace of God and set in motion the powers of redemption."[9]

How can the application of this verse by a wife toward her husband cause him to "safely trust her"?

Now read Proverbs 31:12. A failure common to man is to want to do good only toward those who have first done good to you; but it is contrary to the way of the Lord (Matt. 5:43–45). The Bible tells us of a woman who did "good and not evil" toward her husband, in spite of his actions.

Turn to 1 Samuel 25 and read verses 2–42. Name the husband and wife and describe the characteristics of each of them (vv. 2, 3).

BEHIND THE SCENES

"David and his men had associated with these shepherds when they were in the desert. He had provided them protection and other services in return for food."[10] A feast day was approaching, and David was sure Nabal would share of his bounty (vv. 4–9). Nabal refused and replied with scorn and slander (vv. 10–12). David was infuriated and took four hundred men with swords to pay Nabal a visit (v. 13).

From what was told to Abigail in verses 14–17, and from her actions of verses 18–20, what can you conclude about her?

Do you think this was the first time she had covered for her husband's behavior? Why or why not?

With tact, discretion, and wisdom, Abigail appeased David's anger and pleaded for mercy on behalf of her foolish husband (read verses 23–31). According to this account, does it appear Abigail was a God-fearing woman? Why?

What was David's response to Abigail? (v. 35)

Nabal later died of an apparent heart attack and Abigail eventually became a wife of David. But her loyalty and duty as a wife to Nabal and her faithfulness to do what was right in the eyes of the Lord were beyond reproach. She truly exhibited the qualities of a woman who does her husband "good and not evil."

 FAITH ALIVE

Though Nabal was an extreme case, no husband is without failure or weakness simply because he is a fallen human being. The danger is in allowing the Devil to prey on your natural inclinations to "exaggerate your mate's failures and inadequacies, sow suspicion and jealousy, indulge your self-pity, [or] insist that you deserve something better,"[11] then convince you to act in a manner that would be other than pleasing to God. Decide *today* that you will be a wife who does her husband good; and ask of the Lord whatever you need to enable you to live that out.

Now read Proverbs 31:13–15, 17–19. These verses can best be summed up in a word—"diligence."

Read Acts 18:2, 3, 18, 24–26 and Romans 16:3–5. Describe all the areas of Priscilla's life that, in order to be maintained effectively, required diligence.

What do Proverbs 12:24 and 27 record about diligence?

Though a husband carries the place of rulership in the home, a wife can in another sense "rule" the affairs of her household by her diligence in providing order and a healthy environment for her family, both spiritually and physically.

What does Romans 12:11 cite as important characteristics of a believer?

Now read Hebrews 6:10–12. How is serving the needs of your family with diligence also a way of serving the Lord?

Turn to Ephesians 4:28. How does "willingly works with her hands" (Prov. 31:13) meet the needs of more than just a wife's family?

Serving with diligence may mean not doing what is easy or convenient, but concentrating efforts on doing what will best serve the needs of others. It requires faithfulness and the grace of God to serve in the same manner as did our Lord (Matt. 20:28). But remember that "God is able to make all grace abound toward you, that you, always having all sufficiency in all *things*, may have an abundance for every good work" (2 Cor. 9:8).

Now read Proverbs 31:16. The virtuous woman is honest in her business dealings, and her investments are profitable.

Turn to Acts 18:2, 3. Aquila and Priscilla employed Paul for a time in their place of business. How would this show they were both honest and profitable?

Now look at Proverbs 31:20. Perhaps you noticed that Priscilla opened her home for church meetings in every city in which she and Aquila lived. This certainly was an extension of gracious hospitality to all, including the poor.

Scripture gives us another fine example of a woman sensitive to the needs of those less fortunate. Turn to Acts 9:36–41, and read about Dorcas (Tabitha). She exhibited the spirit of her new-found faith in Christ by "willingly" working "with her hands" (Prov. 31:13) to see that the needs of those less fortunate were met.

Turn to Matthew 25:36–40. What were Jesus' words about such selfless acts done in His name? (v. 40)

What eventually happened to Dorcas (Acts 9:40, 41), and what was the effect on her community? (v. 42)

 FAITH ALIVE

Very few of us will have the opportunity to share the gospel of Jesus Christ before hundreds in a large meeting. But we can impact people for the sake of His kingdom in other practical ways. There are many organizations devoted to helping the "least of these" in the name of the Lord, and most are desperate for volunteers. Check with your church or other local agencies for referrals of places where you can serve. The need may even be as close as next door. What better way to show a neighbor the love of God and the relevancy of the gospel to their world than by serving them as Christ taught us to. Take a moment and write down some practical ways that you will reach out to others this month in the name of the Lord.

Turn back to Proverbs 31 and read verses 21 and 22. The virtuous woman is not concerned about seasons of difficulty or stress that will come, for she has spent time preparing.

Read Acts 18:18, 24–26, and Romans 16:3–5. What difficulties might Priscilla have faced in all her moves, in sharing the gospel, and in holding church in her home at a time when Christians were persecuted and killed for their faith?

Does Scripture ever give the impression that Priscilla complained or resented her service with her husband? What do you perceive her attitude to have been?

Priscilla was obviously a woman of courage, conviction, and faith. And we have seen time and again that these qualities are only developed by time spent in the presence of God. Priscilla was spiritually strong and not thrown by times of difficulty in her life.

It takes great spiritual fortitude to stand in faith and support a husband during times of trial or difficulty. But the woman who has clothed her spirit with the scarlet blood of the Lamb (see Prov. 31:21) will be ready both "in season and out of season."

Turn back to the Book of Proverbs and read 31:23. Scripture is clear on the character traits that qualify a man for leadership. But were you aware that a wife can disqualify her husband from leadership if she does not exhibit qualities established in the Word of God for *her* as well?

Turn to 1 Timothy 3. Summarize the qualifications for an overseer as described in verses 1–7.

"'Blameless' [does not mean] perfect, but one against whom no evil charge can be proved. 'The husband of one wife. . . .' Although the phrase obviously prohibits polygamy . . . the dominant thought is monogamous fidelity, that is . . . a faithful husband. For some, the phrase may refer to prohibiting remarriage after divorce, but Paul's chief concern is the . . . conduct as a husband at the time of his candidacy for office."[12]

What is different about or added to the qualifications for deacons? (vv. 8–10, 12)

Can a husband rule his children and household well without the support and cooperation of his wife? Explain.

What four qualifications must the wife of a church leader exhibit? (v. 11)

       WORD WEALTH

Reverent, *semnos.* Behavior that is dignified, honorable, decent, august, worthy of respect. Leaders in the church should set a good example, displaying a deportment that commands respect. Since *semnos* is used of both husband and wife, an idealistic attractiveness should characterize all Christian couples.[13]

There has already been much study on the importance of controlling the tongue (lesson 5—Miriam) and faithfulness (lesson 7—Ruth). The word "temperate" literally means "to keep sober (as in abstaining from wine), to be circumspect or discreet." But it also encompasses much more. Look up the word "temperate" in a dictionary, and develop a complete definition that you feel best describes the wife of a husband in leadership.

Supporting her husband in leadership provides a wife with the opportunity to either truly excel as the "crown of her husband," or to erode his potential from the inside out (Prov. 12:4).

Now read Proverbs 31:24, 25. The virtuous wife gives herself to things that are worthwhile and profitable, that she might grow in character, reap with rejoicing, and have no regrets.

Read Acts 18:3, 18, 24–26; Romans 16:3–5; and 1 Corinthians 16:19. List as many things as you can find, either directly or by implication, that Priscilla gave herself to that were profitable.

Do you think Priscilla and Aquila would have enjoyed their latter years together? Why or why not?

FAITH ALIVE

One cannot minimize the importance of "sowing and reaping" (Gal. 6:7–9), especially when it comes to being a wife who "sows to the Spirit." What a woman sows *will* be seen later, in such places as: her own character, from sowing in the Word and prayer; in her relationship with her husband, from sowing in love, submission and respect; in her children, from sowing in faithfulness and diligence; or in her relationships with others, from sowing in kindness and service. Sowing is a lifetime process, and one may grow weary. But do not lose heart—for in due season, you *will* reap, and "rejoice in time to come" (Gal. 6:9; Prov. 31:25).

Now read Proverbs 31:26, 27. The importance of wisdom was learned through the life of Deborah (lesson 6). We have also learned that our words have power; but how can kindness be expressed in a life-producing fashion?

Turn to James 3:9, 10. What things ought not to be so? (v. 10)

We hold within our mouths the power to bless others or to curse them, to create life in them or to create death. And since two types of speech cannot come from the same mouth, which type should we choose with our will to speak?

One example of a life-producing blessing is, "I know you can do it. Christ will strengthen you." It includes both *truth* and *encouragement*. Write down at least four more phrases of kindness by which someone in your home could be blessed.

Now read Proverbs 31:28–31. The virtuous wife has raised her children to appreciate godly qualities; she has sowed with words of kindness and will reap praise; she understands that service to others is service to God and requires excellence; she attends to her appearance, but realizes true beauty is a matter of the heart; and her love for God is reflected in everything she does.

 FAITH ALIVE

Read through Proverbs 31:10–31 once again. List as many qualities of godly virtue as you can find that are either given directly ("does him good") or implied (is thrifty). Try to find at least twenty.

Keep this list and choose one per week to either refresh yourself on or to newly incorporate into your life. You can do all things through Christ who strengthens you!

1. *Spirit-Filled Life Bible* (Nashville, TN: Thomas Nelson Publishers, 1991), 924, note on 31:10–31.

2. Ibid., 7, note on 2:18.

3. Ibid., 1489, "Word Wealth: 10:7 joined."

4. Ibid., 8, note on 2:24.

5. Ibid., 1734, "Kingdom Dynamics: Jesus and the Father Model Relationship for Marriage."

6. Ibid.

7. Ibid., 1795, note on 5:24–33.

8. Ibid., 1795, "Kingdom Dynamics: Christ and the Church Model Husband/Wife Relationships."

9. Ibid., 1712, "Kingdom Dynamics: Receiving One Another Is the Way to Oneness."

10. Ibid., 430, note on 25:4–9.

11. Ibid., 1441, "Kingdom Dynamics: Divorce Is a Case of a Heart Hardened Toward God."

12. Ibid., 1843, note on 3:2.

13. Ibid., 1844, "Word Wealth: 3:11 reverent."

Lesson 12/Lydia— Daughter of Hospitality

What comes to mind when you hear the word "hospitality"? Does it conjure up images of lavish table settings and extravagant meals, with meticulous attention to the finest details? Do you feel twinges of guilt or pangs of anxiety when you consider the topic? Or does the idea of someone coming to your home seem too overwhelming to even contemplate?

You are not alone if you share these misconceptions regarding the principle of hospitality. It is a word and a custom that has become distorted by the world's standards of what is "appropriate," and pushed aside as a result of the demands of life in today's culture. It is now an almost obsolete practice, even within the body of Christ.

But what *is* true hospitality, in the biblical sense? And is the concept still relevant for today? Let us look into the lives of the Bible women who understood the principle, to gain insight into the mission and fruit of hospitality.

This study opens with Lydia, a New Testament woman who gave herself to hospitality. Turn in your Bible to Acts 16:13–15, where Lydia is first encountered.

 BEHIND THE SCENES

Lydia was among a small group of people in Philippi who met along the riverside for prayer. "Since Jewish law required the establishment of a synagogue when there was a population of at least ten men in a community, the absence of a synagogue in Philippi indicates a small Jewish population."[1] This little band was later converted, and grew into the church to whom Paul was writing in his letter to the Philippians. They became a body with a strong missionary zeal and a lively spirit of fellowship, and they encouraged and supported Paul's ministry.

According to verse 14, where was Lydia from, and what was her occupation?

In spite of her success and the relatively few Jews in Philippi, what was Lydia's religious status? (v. 14)

Paul and Silas visited the small assembly of worshipers and began to talk to the women (v. 13). What did the Lord do for Lydia when Paul began to speak? (v. 14)

What was the result of Paul's conversation with Lydia, and whom did she tell and bring along with her? (v. 15)

(Though Lydia "worshiped God" (v. 14), she was not a Christian until she received the message of the gospel and believed.)

What did Lydia then ask of Paul and Silas? (v. 15)

In the New King James Version, verse 15 says that Lydia "begged" and "persuaded" Paul and Silas. Why do you think she was so anxious to have these men of God in her home?

Paul continues on in Philippi, where he encounters a girl with a "spirit of divination" and casts the spirit out of her (v. 18). Read Acts 16:16–39 to discover what followed.

According to Acts 16:40, where did Paul and Silas finally end up?

Imagine for a moment that you are Lydia, or a member of her household. How do you think it felt to hear firsthand the account of Paul and Silas's imprisonment, subsequent miraculous release, and their other experiences?

What do you think their testimony did for Lydia and those who were with her?

Verse 40 tells us that Paul and Silas departed. Do you think Lydia's door continued to be open to believers needing a place to stay? Why or why not?

Now turn to Philippians 1:1–11, where Paul, chained in a prison cell, is writing to his friends back in Philippi, among whom is Lydia. Considering his difficult circumstances, why do you think his remembrance of them brought him such joy? (v. 4)

Why do you think he longs for them all? (v. 8)

What can you conclude about the ministry of Lydia to Paul by means of her gracious hospitality?

⚔ WORD WEALTH

Hospitality, *philoxenos.* To entertain strangers, be fond of guests, given to (lover of) hospitality. From the root word *philos,* meaning a friend or neighbor; fondly, friendly.

We have already seen (in lesson 11) the gracious and loving way Priscilla extended hospitality not only to Paul (Acts 18:3), but also to the many others who were part of the churches she and Aquila led in their homes (Rom. 16:3–5; 1 Cor. 16:19).

This principle was illustrated in this decade, long after Priscilla applied it, in a once-small congregation that was growing rapidly through the ministry of hospitality. In this particular church, visitors were acknowledged during the service, then greeted afterward by various church members. These members (volunteers who came prepared) then invited the visitor and their family to their homes for lunch. Not all visitors accepted; but among those who did, there were powerful testimonies of salvations and future church participation.

Since the word "hospitality" is found in the Bible only in the New Testament, **was the practice then limited to the early church? Did it really apply either before or after that time?**

Turn to Exodus 23:9. What was the Lord's command regarding the treatment of "strangers"? (Notice "stranger" is also translated "sojourner.")

Now turn to Leviticus 19:34. What additional command was given that pertained to strangers?

"God indicates that He expects us to relate to strangers in deep, unselfish, servant-spirited, Christian love. He reminds His people that they, who once were foreigners in the land of Egypt, should above all others remember how it feels to be treated as outsiders. . . . [Though] opposite to normal, worldly standards. . . strangers . . . are to be treated as 'one born among you,' that is, as blood relatives."[2]

How does God feel about strangers? (Deut. 10:18)

What unusual thing does Hebrews 13:2 reveal about entertaining strangers?

 KINGDOM EXTRA

For an actual example of what is mentioned in Hebrews 13:2, review the incident involving Abraham and Sarah in Genesis 18:1–15.

The principle of hospitality is clearly evident, if not in actual word then certainly in deed, throughout the Old Testament, as well as the New. (Read 2 Kin. 4:8–37 for the story of Elisha and the Shunammite woman.) Both Lydia and the Shunammite woman were apparently blessed with an abundance of resources, used wisely for the sake of God's kingdom. **But is abundance a necessary prerequisite for providing hospitality?**

Turn back in your Bible to 1 Kings 17 and read verses 10–24.

 BEHIND THE SCENES

When the land of Israel became unsafe for the prophet Elijah, the Lord sent His servant to the city of Zarephath, in Sidon. This was the native land of his wicked enemy, Jezebel (of whom we learned in lesson 11), who had put a price on his head and had many looking for him. Yet, as Elijah entered the gates of the city, he was led by the Lord to a righteous widow. The land at the time was in the midst of a terrible drought, and the widow and her son were in the throes of its effect.

What was Elijah's first request of the widow of Zarephath? (v. 10)

She went to get it, but was halted by his next question. What did he then ask from her? (v. 11)

The woman then explained her desperate condition to Elijah. What were his first three words to her? (v. 13)

Of what might she have been afraid?

What was Jesus' command to those with similar worries? (Matt. 6:25–34)

What was the widow's faith-filled, "kingdom-seeking" response to the prophet Elijah's request? (1 Kin. 17:15)

According to the promise in Matthew 6:33, what was "added unto" the widow of Zarephath? (vv. 15, 16)

"The woman overcame her fear, responded in faith, and God was faithful to His promise,"[3] making provision for the widow, her son, and Elijah for over two years.

What additional blessing did the widow of Zarephath receive as a result of her hospitality to Elijah? Read 1 Kings 17:17–24, and summarize that account.

One never knows whom the Lord would desire to bring into your life, and what blessing or "divine coincidence" may come as a result of your hospitality.

A more recent woman of hospitality, Myrene, discovered this to be true when, many years ago, she heard of a South African pastor/evangelist and his family who were led of the Lord to visit and minister in Los Angeles. Myrene and her husband felt prompted to host them, and the two families became knit together during their three-week stay in Myrene's home. Who, but God, could have known that seventeen years later, a son of that same evangelist would come to visit, fall in love with, and marry Myrene's daughter, and the two of them would enter ministry together? The Lord can certainly bless through the ministry of hospitality.

So we have seen that hospitality is a principle evident throughout the Bible, is used by God for mutual blessing, and should not be hindered by one's natural ability to provide it. **But are only certain people called to the ministry of hospitality?**

Review the Word Wealth entry on hospitality. Included in the meanings are "lover of hospitality" and "fond of guests." Hence, there *are* those who are specifically gifted to host others. But just as intercessors being anointed for prayer doesn't exclude the rest of us from praying, neither is hospitality to be left for those to whom it comes more naturally.

Turn to both 1 Timothy 3:2 and Titus 1:7, 8. What specific groups were required to be hospitable?

Now turn to Romans 12:9–21. Paul is exhorting *all* believers to show true Christian love through a number of duties. Which of these are mentioned in verses 13 and 20?

(Notice "given to" is also translated "pursuing.")

Turn now to 1 Peter 4:8–11, where believers are asked to show "fervent love for one another." What is included as one expression of that fervency? (v. 9)

According to 1 Timothy 5:10, what are listed as the "good works" of a widow?

In summary, record who is to be given to hospitality and who is exempt.

It is clear that hospitality is a form of ministry in which God desires every believer to participate. **But to whom are we to reach out with the ministry of hospitality?**

In our study thus far, we have seen how God used the hospitality of the saints to bless His full-time servants. How does 3 John 5–7 confirm that this is a worthy effort?

What is said of those who support God's messengers? (v. 8)

It is evident from what has already been studied that believers should also show hospitality to one another (1 Pet. 4:9–11; 1 Tim. 3:2). This priority is most clearly seen in the fact that the early church actually began by people opening their homes (Acts 2:46; 20:20; 1 Cor. 16:19). Give some of the reasons why believers need the fellowship of one another.

Turn now to Luke 14:12–14. List those whom Jesus said *not* to include when you open your home (v. 12).

Whom **does** He ask believers to invite into their homes?
(v. 13)

Obviously, Jesus did not intend for us to exclude those we
know from fellowship in our homes. The point is to be motivated by what we can *give* to people in need, not by what we
will *get* from those who have resources. "Reward that will not
be returned in the present age will be given 'at the resurrection of the just'. . . . In the future age, God will reward those
who have been merciful in this age."[4]

In Matthew 25:35–40, Jesus taught an important lesson
about the giving of our resources to those less fortunate. How
was that summarized in verse 40?

"How may we know our Lord? We know Him in doing
His works and in doing them as much to Him as for Him. We
know Him by putting our arms around those who are desperate or alone. He said that when we do this we are putting our
arms around Him—Jesus Christ, our blessed Savior."[5]

God desires us to "be His hands extended," and to reach
out to those who are in particular need of His embrace. How
does Psalm 68:5, 6 show us one of the means by which we can
accomplish this?

Review the entire lesson thus far and summarize the specific groups of people whom the Lord desires us to reach out
to and care for through the ministry of hospitality.

**What does it actually mean to be hospitable to some-
one? Are there guidelines in Scripture for what one is to do?**

Look first at Luke 19:1–6. Zacchaeus has the opportunity to host Jesus in his home. How does verse 6 say he received Him?

The word "joyfully" used here literally means "calmly happy, well-off, glad, rejoicing." What a wonderful guideline for receiving others into your home. It is a joy and a privilege to reach out in the name of the Lord, and it is something we should approach calmly and naturally, without stress or pretense.

Look now at Mark 9:41. What small token does Jesus use as an example of reaching out in Jesus' name?

Hospitality does not require extravagance or abundance. Sometimes, the simplest of expressions (for example, a cup of coffee, or a soft drink) when done with the love and compassion of Christ, are far more meaningful to someone than a huge display. In the case of biblical hospitality, it is truly the thought that counts.

Turn now in your Bible to Luke 10:2–8. Jesus was providing instructions to those He was sending forth in ministry. What does He tell them in verses 7 and 8?

It is clear that the point of providing for people through hospitality was simply to give them *sustenance*, enough food to sustain their health and give them strength. It did not have to be fancy food or presented in masterful style. The power of hospitality, like the gospel, is in its practical simplicity: the *Bread of Life* and the *Living Water* (John 4:10; 6:48).

Now read Matthew 26:26–30. Jesus Himself took the opportunity of fellowship over a meal to communicate one of the most powerful yet intimate truths He ever conveyed to His disciples—that of His redemptive sacrifice. "A new and living way into the presence and provision of God was being prepared through Christ, the Lamb of God."[6] There is power when believers share in the "breaking of bread," for every time we eat and drink, we remember Christ's provision for us, and can use the ministry of hospitality to share that truth with others.

Finally, turn to Luke 10:38–42, and read this passage.

BEHIND THE SCENES

"Martha and Mary were sisters who lived in the village of Bethany, a suburb of Jerusalem. It appears Martha was the elder, for verse 38 speaks of Martha's receiving Jesus 'into her house.' Thus, Martha felt more keenly the domestic responsibilities of keeping house and the demands of providing hospitality."[7]

Martha was caring for the needs of her guests, but what does verse 39 indicate by the word "also" that Martha sometimes did?

How does verse 40 show that Mary did more than just sit at Jesus' feet?

We can conclude from this that the problem was not that Martha was always serving and Mary was "too spiritually minded to be any earthly good." What was the real issue that Jesus was addressing? Look in verse 41 and record His first statement to Martha.

WORD WEALTH

Worry, *merimnao.* From *merizo,* "to divide into parts."
The word suggests a distraction, a preoccupation with things
causing anxiety, stress, and pressure.[8]

Obviously, Martha was allowing herself to become far too
preoccupied and stressed with the details of serving her guests
and was perhaps feeling pressured that everything was not
"just so." In verse 42, Jesus so lovingly reminds her of what is
actually valuable and worthwhile: *the giving and receiving of
ministry.* That is also the guiding principle behind biblical hospitality. It is doubtful whether people will remember what they
ate, or how it was served, months after leaving your home. But
they will always remember what they came away with in their
hearts.

Hospitality is a joyous way to extend the life of Christ to
others in the comfort and intimacy of your own home. It can
be a stretch in many ways, for it is not always convenient, it
may not go as you planned, and you may be required to
receive those who are in a rather unlovable condition, whether
spiritually, emotionally, or physically. But consider our model,
the Lord Jesus Christ, who so lovingly and willingly, with
humble graciousness, reached toward us in spite of our unwor-
thiness, and extended to us the hope of eternal life.

1. *Spirit-Filled Life Bible* (Nashville, TN: Thomas Nelson Publishers, 1991), 1658,
note on 16:13.
2. Ibid., 172, "Kingdom Dynamics: Unselfish Christian Love Toward Strangers."
3. Ibid., 514, note on 17:8–15.
4. Ibid., 1543, note on 14:14.
5. Ibid., 1455, "Kingdom Dynamics: All of Our Giving Is to Be as to God Our
Source."
6. Ibid., 1457, "Kingdom Dynamics: God Sovereignly Inaugurates the New
Covenant."
7. Ibid., 1534, "Kingdom Dynamics: Balancing Devotion and Duty (Martha and
Mary)."
8. Ibid., 1415, "Word Wealth: 6:25 worry."

A Final Word to God's Daughters

In the first lesson of "Biblical Ministries Through Women: God's Daughters and God's Work," we realized that the primary purpose for opening the Bible and examining the lives of its women was twofold: 1) to discover the *truth* of God's Word as it relates to women and 2) to discover how that truth applies to God's daughters today—to you and me. I hope your study has provided the beginning point for a lifelong pursuit of revelation through Scripture, application of truth, and transformation of the heart that you might be fully prepared for all that God would do in and through you (2 Tim. 3:14–17).

There were principles lightly touched upon in this study guide that are fundamental to understanding and applying what you have learned. Hence, we will take a closer and final look at these foundational truths to ensure they are settled in your understanding.

First, receive the truth that *you are* God's Daughter!

If you believe in His Son (John 3:16) and have given your life to becoming a true disciple (Luke 14:33), then you are *His* (1 Cor. 6:19, 20). Nothing can change that or separate you from God's love (Rom. 8:38, 39). The King of the Universe is your Father, and you *are*—now—a daughter of royal lineage (Gal. 4:7; 1 Pet. 2:9, 10). As such, you can walk in the confidence of the full authority provided by His kingship.

Second, you are one of "His own special people" (1 Pet. 2:9). The promises of God through His Word are *yours* to receive (2 Cor. 1:20; 2 Pet. 1:2–4). The only condition is your continued faithfulness and loving obedience to all He has called you to as a follower of the living Lord (Deut. 28:1–14). Although all of us will stumble and fall short of His glory (Rom. 3:23), the Lord Jesus has made provision for our failure through His cross (Rom. 3:24–26). We must simply confess our sin and be cleansed and restored (1 John 1:9); then, forgetting the past, continue ahead toward His upward call (Phil. 3:13, 14). This transforming work is a process that requires daily choices to live life on God's terms; but it is not a burdensome task, for He enables you by His grace and the power of His Spirit to walk according to God's will for you (Zech. 4:6; 2 Cor. 12:9).

Third, remember that God has a plan and purpose for your life. Believe that! It is far above what you would even ask or think (Eph. 3:20, 21). His requirement of you is simply to be available to all He would do through you. He *will not* give up on you (Phil. 1:6). He is continually at work in your life (Phil. 2:13) and will complete in you all that you commit to Him. As Rahab discovered, His purpose for you does not depend upon your heritage, your past, or your ability to qualify but solely upon His forgiveness, grace, and love as the Great Redeemer and All-Mighty God (1 Cor. 5:7; Heb. 13:20, 21; 1 John 1:9).

Finally, are you willing to leave behind anything and everything that might hinder God's best for you? This broad realm can include failure, success, inadequacy, fear, desire, unforgiveness, plans, or pain. Will you instead reach forward with faith, righteousness, and the resurrection power of God to fully embrace all that He would do in and through your life, for the furtherance of His kingdom, and the glory of His name? (Phil. 3:13, 14; 1 Pet. 4:11).

So let's advance in that grace—together! If you are willing to take His hand and be led into His complete purpose for you, regardless of cost, STOP right now. Let's *both* pray. And as we do, tell the Lord Jesus that very thing: "Jesus, lead me into Your full purpose for me. I surrender to it."

Once you make that decision, you will be satisfied with nothing less than God's highest calling for you. And, like Mary, follow Him *always,* from your heart, saying, "Behold the maidservant of the Lord! Let it be to me according to your word" (Luke 1:38).